For the Breasts of Friends

A collection of favorite recipes —
some new, some handed down from mothers and
grandmothers and some shared by good friends.

Women working for a cure.

"*I am only one, but still I am one,
I cannot do everything but still I can do
something; I will not refuse to do the
something I can do.*"   *Helen Keller*

Written and published by
Breast Friends Publishing
Box 436, Foam Lake, SK. Canada S0A 1A0
Printed by Gateway Publishing Co. Ltd.
385 DeBaets Street Winnipeg R2J 4J8
Ph: 222-4294 1-800-665-4878 Fx: 224-4410
Cover design — Laurel Ostapowich, Elfros SK.
Photography by Backyard Studios, Foam Lake
All accessories and props supplied by
Golden Ocean Giftware
Foam Lake, SK.
Copyright @2004 by Breast Friends Publishing

Canadian Cataloguing in Publication Data

Main entry under title:
For the Breasts of Friends

Includes index.
ISBN 0-9735239-0-5

1. Cookery I. Breast Friends

TX714.C44 2004   641.5   C04-900651-9

Sixth Printing — 2005

Introduction
The Breast Friends

The Breast Friends are a group of menopausal women from a small Saskatchewan community that, like most women, have been affected by breast cancer in their families, friends or colleagues. In the summer of 2003, after a scare with her own health and the loss of some very special people, Linda Helgason decided to ride with the Prairie Women on Snowmobiles to raise money for breast cancer research. Nine friends jumped on board to act as her fundraising committee and became *Breast Friends*. Nat Dunlop, Val Helgason, Jeannie Johnson, Jacquie Klebeck, Charlene Rokochy, Darlene Cooper, Cecile Halyk, Anne Reynolds and Patti Hack decided to host a banquet in their small rural community, Foam Lake, Saskatchewan. Their goal was to help Linda raise three thousand dollars. Well, the banquet was a great success to say the least. With the help of community sponsors, and a warm, caring community, the goal of three thousand soon turned into five thousand and in the final counting, Linda headed off to ride with Prairie Women on Snowmobiles, with the largest contribution ever---over eighteen thousand dollars. During the banquet and for many days after, the committee was asked for copies of the recipes for the dishes that they served. Another idea blossomed. "Let's publish a book with the banquet recipes, and a collection of our favorite recipes, and make some more money for breast cancer research." So, once Christmas was over and all of our families had gone home- the work began - this book is the result and we hope you enjoy it as much as we enjoyed putting it together. Share it with your mothers, daughters, granddaughters, sisters and all the important women in your life. Let's pray that the next generation of women talk about breast cancer as a disease of the past.

Linda on her ride.

Dedication

To those who are missed every day.
The angels among us

Hazel
Wilkins

Olga
Stuckel

Reena
Campbell
Partridge

Avra
Teplitsky

And to every woman that has lost the
fight against breast cancer,

&
to a future where no one
has to face this devastating disease.

"There is no more creative force in the world than menopausal women with zest." Margaret Mead

"The ten women that have compiled these recipes collectively have 33 children, 42 grandchildren, and 322 years of marital experience. We have no doubt that together, they could move mountains!'

The husbands and cookbook widowers!

Table of Contents

*Recipes.that were served at our breast cancer banquet can be identified by their names which all include "The Breast....."

Appetizers

"Good food ends with good talk."
Geoffrey Neighbor

Whether you are serving appetizers or having a
Tapas Party, these recipes are great ones to try.
These are some of the terms used for these dishes.

Appetizers - small serving of food or beverage served before
or as the first course of a meal.

Hors d'oeuvres- Small savory appetizers served before the
meal, customarily with appetizers or cocktails. They are
usually one or two-bite size and can be cold or hot.

Dim sum- Cantonese for heart's delight, dim sum includes a
variety of small, mouth-watering dishes such as steamed or
fried dumplings, shrimp balls, steamed buns and pastries

Tapas Popular throughout Spain in bars and restaurants.
Tapas are appetizers that usually accompany sherry or other
apéritifs or cocktails. They can also form an entire meal and
can range from simple items such as olives or cubes of ham
and cheese to more elaborate preparations like snails in a
spicy sauce, stuffed peppers and miniature sandwiches.

Canapés - Garnished bite-sized rounds of bread or
vegetables served with cocktails and at buffets.

Crudités - French word for an American cocktail appetizer
of raw vegetables served with a dip.

Pupus- Hawaiian appetizers or snack foods.

BAKED CHICKEN WINGS

½ cup flour
2 pounds chicken wings
1 cup white sugar
½ cup vinegar
3 tablespoons soya sauce
3 tablespoons water
½ teaspoon seasononq salt

Cut chicken wings at the joint, removing the ends. Place flour in a plastic bag and shake chicken wings in flour to coat. Brown wings in oil in frying pan.
Combine all other ingredients in a sauce pan over medium heat. Heat until sugar dissolves. Pour mixture over wings and bake at 350°F. for one hour, basting every 20 minutes.

Making a "living" is not the same as making a "life."

BAKED SPINACH LOAF

1 round pumpernickel bread
1 package chopped frozen spinach
1 package Knorr cream of vegetable soup mix
¾ cup sour cream
1 cup mayonnaise
2 cups shredded marble cheese
5 ounce can water chestnuts drained and chopped fine
small white onion chopped fine

Combine soup mix, sour cream and mayonnaise well.
Drain and pat dry thawed spinach, add to bowl. Add
onion and chestnuts mixing well. Blend in grated cheese.
Hollow out bread saving the top and inside bread. Place
mixture inside bread and fit the top back on. Completely
wrap the loaf in foil and bake in preheated 350° F.
oven for 1 hour. Serve with remaining bread, crackers
or taco chips.

**You can tell a lot about a person by the way he
handles three things; a rainy day, lost luggage
and tangled Christmas tree lights.**

BARBECUED CHICKEN WINGS

(A favorite at the cabin at the lake.)

3 pounds fresh chicken wings

sprinkle with salt, pepper or seasoning salt

½ cup ketchup

2 tablespoons honey

½ teaspoon garlic

dash chili pepper

Cut chicken wings at joint removing the ends. Season well with salt, pepper or seasoning salt. On medium barbecue, cook wings until crispy and cooked through. Serve with the simple dipping sauce.

Sauce for dipping: Blend ketchup and honey and seasoning in a small bowl. Can be doubled if more sauce is required.

WINTER WINGS:

When the barbecue is covered with snow we adopt this recipe:

Cut chicken wings at joint removing the ends.

Combine and pour over chicken:

1 cup honey

½ cup soya

2 tablespoons ketchup

1 clove garlic crushed

Bake at 350° F. for 50 minutes.

3

THE "BREAST" CRAB ROLLS
(Make the day ahead, so it slices better
and holds together.)
1 pound crab flavored seafood
16 ounces French onion dip
(Heluva Good Dip from Costco works well)
8 tortilla wraps
Flake the crab into small pieces and mix with the dip.
Spread onto the tortillas and roll up. Cover and place
in the fridge overnight. Cut each roll into about 8
pieces.

BRUSCHETTA
½ cup tomato, chopped
½ cup onion, chopped
½ cup green or black olives, chopped
salt and pepper
½ teaspoon oregano
¼ teaspoon garlic powder
2 tablespoons mayonnaise
1 cup mozzarella cheese, grated
Mix and spread mixture over sliced baguette rounds.
Bake at 375° F. until heated and cheese is melted .

COCONUT CHEESE BALL

This cheeseball is not only delicious, but also visually appealing with flecks of red and green sprinkled throughout. May be enjoyed anytime but it suits the Christmas season with its color and "snowball" appearance.

1 package cream cheese (250 ml)
1 – 2 green onions, chopped
3 – 4 radishes, chopped
Sweet flaked coconut

Add the chopped green onions and radish to the cheese; work quickly and form into a ball, then roll in sweet flaked coconut. Serve with crackers.

It is Beautiful Woman Month and tag, you are it!

CHEESE DIPS

VEGGIE CHEESE DIP

1 cup mayonnaise

¾ cup cheddar cheese, shredded

1 cup sour cream

5 teaspoons onion flakes

1 teaspoon dill

2 teaspoons parsley flakes

1 teaspoon lemon pepper

Mix all together and serve with veggies or crackers. Extra sour cream can be added if you like a lighter consistency.

SALSA AND CHEESE DIP

1 cup mayonnaise

1 cup sour cream

1 cup medium salsa

2 cups cheddar cheese, grated

In a mixing bowl blend mayonnaise, sour cream and salsa. Stir in cheese. Serve with taco chips. You may add extra cheese or vary the type of salsa depending on whether you like it mild or hot.

CRAB STUFFED MUSHROOMS

12 large mushrooms
6 ounce frozen crab meat
3 tablespoons plain dry bread crumbs
3 dashes hot pepper sauce
2 tablespoons butter or margarine, melted
1 envelope vegetable soup mix
½ cup sour cream or plain yogurt
1 tablespoon snipped fresh dill weed
⅛ teaspoon pepper

Preheat oven to 350° F. Remove and finely chop
mushroom stems. Combine chopped mushroom stems,
vegetable soup mix, crab meat, sour cream or plain
yogurt, bread crumbs, dill, hot pepper sauce and pepper
in a medium bowl. Arrange mushroom caps on a lightly
greased baking sheet. Stuff with crabmeat mixture and
then brush with butter.
Bake for 15 min or until tender.
Makes about 12 appetizers. Yield: 4 servings.
*Mushrooms can be prepared one day in advance.
Simply prepare and stuff as above. Cover and
refrigerate. To serve, brush with butter and then bake as
above.

CRAB-FILLED APPETIZER LOAF

2 -8 ounce packages cream cheese
1 cup green onion, chopped
1 cup mayonnaise
2 teaspoons dill weed
1 tin crab meat
1 cup cheddar cheese, grated
½ cup bacon bits (real bacon)
1 loaf of French bread

Mix all ingredients. Slice the top off of a French loaf of bread and hollow out a cavity in the loaf large enough to hold the above mixture. Fill cavity with crab mixture, cover with the "top" that you had sliced off. Wrap with foil and bake for 1 ½ hours at 350°F.
Use bread "pieces" removed from the loaf for dipping.

God put me on this earth to accomplish a certain number of things. Right now I am so far behind, I will live forever.

THE BREAST HOT MUSHROOM TARTS

8 ounces cream cheese, softened

1 ½ cups flour

½ cup butter or margarine softened

¾ pound fresh mushrooms, chopped

1 large onion, finely chopped

1 teaspoon salt

pepper to taste

¼ cup sour cream

2 teaspoons flour

Mix cream cheese, flour and butter together; cover and let stand for 1 hour.
In a non-stick skillet, using a small amount of butter, cook mushrooms and onion until soft. Season with salt and pepper. Add flour and sour cream.
Roll out dough and cut to fit small tart shells.
Fill about two thirds full with mushroom mixture.
Bake in preheated 350° F. until shells are golden brown, about 10 to 15 minutes.

Makes 48 tarts

HAM TURNOVERS
(A favorite at Christmas time.)

Use a favorite pie crust dough.

Mix together:
1½ cups cooked ground ham
½ cup mushroom soup
2 tablespoons pickles or olives, chopped
1 tablespoon onion, chopped
1½ tablespoons ketchup
salt & pepper if needed

Roll to the thickness of ⅛ inch pie crust dough. Cut into 2½ inch rounds. Place in the center of each round as much filling as will fit. Moisten edges with water; fold over and pinch together with fork. Place crescents on a cookie sheet and brush lightly with 1 egg yolk mixed with 2 tablespoons cream. Poke tops with fork several times. Bake at 400° F. for about 20 minutes or until dough is done.

HOT ZUCCHINI SQUARES

(A wonderful contrast to the sweets served at coffee time.)

3 cups zucchini, very thinly sliced

¼ cup onion, minced

2 tablespoons parsley, chopped

½ teaspoon leaf oregano

¾ teaspoon salt

1 clove garlic, minced

½ cup Parmesan cheese, grated

4 eggs, slightly beaten

1 cup flour

1 ½ teaspoons baking powder

½ teaspoon seasoned salt

⅛ teaspoon black pepper

1 tablespoon butter, melted

½ cup canola oil

In a large bowl mix zucchini, onion, parsley, oregano, salt, garlic and cheese. Stir in eggs and mix well. In a small bowl combine flour, baking powder, seasoned salt and pepper. Mix well into zucchini mixture, then add melted butter and oil. Pour into a 9x13-inch greased pan. Bake at 350°F, for 25 minutes or until golden. Cut in squares and serve warm. This freezes well.

CHEESE AND ASPARAGUS PUFF

4 large or 5 medium eggs

2 cups milk

½ teaspoon salt

pinch of pepper

1 cup fine cracker crumbs

10 ounces Edam or Gouda cheese cut into ¼ inch cubes

1 pound fresh asparagus, cut into ½ inch pieces

2 tablespoons butter, melted

Into large casserole break eggs and beat with whisk.

Add all remaining ingredients except asparagus and butter.

Stir until thoroughly blended.

Arrange asparagus on top- drizzle over melted butter.

Bake at 350° F. for 50-60 minutes.

Serves 6.

"Happy people evaluate themselves, unhappy people evaluate others."

LAYERED TACO DIP

8 ounces cream cheese, softened
½ cup sour cream
1 cup salsa, hot or mild
½ cup green onions, chopped
½ cup iceberg lettuce, shredded
4 tomatoes, chopped
1 ½ cups cheddar cheese shredded
½ cup black olives, sliced

Beat cream cheese and sour cream together until
smooth.
Spread evenly in bottom of 9" dish or glass pie plate.
Spread salsa over cream cheese layer.
Sprinkle evenly with onions, then lettuce, tomatoes,
cheese and olives.
Serve with tortilla chips or pita chips.

*"I think men who have a pierced ear are better prepared
for marriage. They've experienced pain and
bought jewelry."*   *Rita Rudner*

FAMOUS HOT BROCCOLI CHEESE DIP
(Sinfully good, don't try counting the
calories- just enjoy!)

1 pound butter
1 large onion, chopped
1 pound Velvetta cheese
2 – 3 teaspoons garlic powder
1 package frozen broccoli, thawed and drained
2 cans sliced mushrooms, drained
2 cans mushroom soup
¼ cup slivered almonds
1 round loaf sour-dough bread

Sauté onions in butter. Add next 6 ingredients.
Stir until cheese is melted. Fill hollowed out loaf
with cheese mixture. Reserve removed bread for
dipping. Replace top on loaf, wrap in foil and
bake for one hour at 350° F. This filling is
enough for two loaves. Use half and freeze the
other half for another celebration.

**Amazing!!!! You hang something in your closet
for awhile, and it shrinks two sizes!!!**

14

YULETIDE APPETIZER LOG
(An attractive and delicious appetizer.)

1 - 8 ounce package cream cheese
¼ cup margarine or salad dressing
2 tablespoons lemon juice
2 hard boiled eggs
2 cups cooked chicken or turkey, finely sliced
¼ cup green onion, sliced
½ teaspoon salt
¼ teaspoon ginger
⅛ teaspoon pepper
4 drops red pepper sauce

Mix all the ingredients together. Place on a platter and shape into the form of a log. Garnish with sesame seeds, green pepper or green onion, red pepper, and/or pitted black olives.
Add variations according to taste. Serve with crackers.

An English professor wrote the words, "Woman without her man is nothing," on the blackboard and directed the students to punctuate it properly.
The men wrote: "Woman, without her man, is nothing. The women wrote: "Woman! Without her, man is nothing."

FRESH VEGETABLE PIZZA
(What would we do without cream cheese?)

2-8 ounce packages Pillsbury crescent rolls

1-8 ounce package cream cheese

¾ cup mayonnaise

1 tablespoon ranch dressing

broccoli	carrots
green pepper	green onions
cauliflower	red pepper
celery	olives

Heat oven to 375°F. Separate dough into 4 long triangles. Place rectangles crosswise in ungreased 15x10" jellyroll pan; press over bottom and 1" up sides to form crust. Seal perforations. Bake for 10-12 minutes or until golden brown. Cool completely.

In small bowl, beat cream cheese until smooth. Add mayonnaise, ranch dressing and blend until smooth. Spread evenly over cooled crust. Chop finely, and sprinkle veggies evenly on top. Cut into 60 appetizer pieces. Refrigerate leftovers.

* Note: vegetable choices and amounts vary according to your taste.

POPEYE BAKE

Spray quiche tins with non stick spray.

Beat 3 eggs

Combine: 1 cup flour

        ½ teaspoon salt

        1 teaspoon baking powder

Add to beaten eggs.

Add 2½ cups medium cheddar, grated, to 4 cups spinach, washed and chopped.

If it is summer and you have access to fresh spices, add to the above mixture:

½ cup green onions, chopped

¼ cup dill, chopped

2 tablespoons green tops of garlic, chopped

¼ cup parsley, chopped

or for the Winter Variation add to the spinach and cheese:

¼ cup onion, minced

1 teaspoon dried basil

1 teaspoon dried oregano

¼ teaspoon garlic powder

¼ cup parsley, chopped

Mix egg mixture with spinach, cheese and either fresh or winter herbs. Fill quiche tins ⅔ full and bake at 325° F. for 15-20 minutes.

JERK PORK SKEWERS

1 pound pork tenderloin

1 teaspoon salt

½ teaspoon black pepper

3 teaspoons garlic powder

2 tablespoons onion powder

½ cup jerk sauce (commercial or recipe that follows)

6 to 8 tablespoons olive oil

Cut pork tenderloin into 1-inch cubes. In a bowl, combine salt, pepper, garlic powder, onion powder, jerk sauce and olive oil. Marinade pork for a minimum of 4 hours to overnight. Preheat oven to 350° F. or preheat grill to medium high. Thread pork cubes onto small wooden skewers. Bake for 10 to 15 minutes in oven or grill over medium heat, about 10 minutes. While cooking turn once and baste with marinade until well browned. Serves 4 as tapas or an appetizer.

Mid-life is when the growth of hair on our legs slows down. This gives us plenty of time to care for our newly acquired mustache.

CARRIBEAN JERK SAUCE

5 minced green onions
¼ cup fresh orange juice
1 tablespoon minced ginger
½ minced jalapeno pepper
1 tablespoon lime juice
1 tablespoon Soya sauce
1 teaspoon minced garlic
1 teaspoon ground allspice
¼ teaspoon cinnamon
½ teaspoon ground cloves
Combine green onions, orange juice, ginger, hot
pepper, lemon or lime juice, soy sauce, garlic, allspice,
cinnamon and cloves. Makes a wonderful marinade for
pork or chicken.

*"After all of these years, I see that I was mistaken about
Eve in the beginning; it is better to live outside the
Garden with her, than inside it without her." Mark Twain*

MUSHROOM SPINACH ROLL

(These are delicious sliced into rounds and served with a salad for lunch, or served as an appetizer.)

Thaw package of phyllo frozen pastry - 2 hours

2 tablespoons butter	1 large onion, diced
½ pound mushrooms	1 bunch spinach
3 tablespoons parsley	⅛ teaspoon nutmeg
3 eggs, beaten	¼ cup Parmesan cheese

¼ cup Swiss or Mozzarella cheese, grated

3 tablespoons butter

Melt first amount of butter in pan. Sauté onion in butter, and when onion is transparent add sliced mushrooms and continue cooking. Clean and cut ends off of one bunch of spinach. Add to pan until barely wilted. Let cool and mix in parsley, nutmeg, eggs and cheeses.

Melt second amount of butter (3 tablespoons).

On counter lay out one sheet of phyllo and brush with melted butter. Add next sheet and brush until you have 5 in a stack. Spoon spinach mixture down the long side of phyllo. Roll up and turn seam down on a buttered pan. Brush outside with butter. Bake at 375° F. for 30 to 40 minutes. Re-wrap left over phyllo and store in fridge, it will stay good for about 1 week.

SHRIMP MOUSSE

1 -8 ounce package cream cheese

1 envelope unflavored gelatin

¼ cup water

1 -10 ounce can tomato soup

½ cup celery, chopped fine

parsley to taste

1 cup green onion, chopped

1 cup mayonnaise

2 cups shrimp

Mash cheese; heat over low heat in soup till hot.
Mix envelope of gelatin in water and add to soup.
Allow this mixture to cool completely. Add the rest
of the veggies, mayonnaise, shrimp, and refrigerate.
Serve with crackers. Note: Can be frozen.

CRAB MOUSSE

Melt together.

1 can mushroom soup

1 -8 ounce package cream cheese

Add: 1½ cups crab

¼ cup celery, chopped

¼ cup green onions, chopped

1 cup mayonnaise

1 package unflavoured gelatin mixed in ¼ cup hot
water. Mix and pour in decorative bowl or mold and
chill before serving. Serve with favorite crackers.

PITA CHIPS
(low fat crunchy chips)

3 pita pockets
Seasoning salt (or seasoning of your choice)

Cut pita pockets in half, then cut each half into 3 triangle pieces. Pull the pieces apart and lay them inside surface up on a cookie sheet. Sprinkle with Seasoning salt.
Bake at 200° for 10 minutes. Serves 4.

Did you know how much a woman's chance of getting breast cancer increases as she gets older?

By age 30....   1 out of 2,525
By age 40...   1 out of 217
By age 50...   1 out of 50
By age 60...   1 out of 24
By age 70...   1 out of 14
By age 80...   1 out of 10
Ever ...   1 out of 8

Source: Northwestern Ontario Breast Screening Program; Canadian Cancer Society

Beverages

"A woman is like a teabag — only in hot water do you realize how strong she is."
Nancy Reagan

CRAB APPLE LIQUEUR
(This has been said to make a women
see double and feel single.)

1 pound red crab apples (approximately) per
quart jar
1 cup sugar per quart jar
2 cups vodka (approximately) per quart jar

Wash and remove stems from the ripe red crab
apples. Cut into quarters. Pack into quart jars
up to an inch from the top. Add 1 cup of sugar
to each jar. Pour the vodka over the apples and
sugar until it just reaches the surface. Seal the
jars. Place the sealed jars on their sides in a
cool storage room. Turn once a day for 25 to
28 days. Then strain the liquid through a sieve
and again through a fine strainer. When you
are satisfied with its clarity, bottle in clean gin or
vodka bottles. For a clearer drink, you may
want to decant it after a few days. Do not throw
away the pulp, but put it back into the jars, and
carefully pour off the remaining liquid.
Eventually when there is very little settling out,
you can discard the pulp.

CITRUS SLUSH

(Find a few good friends, set out some lawn chairs on the shores of Fishing Lake and enjoy!)

4 cups sugar
8 cups water

6 cups unsweetened orange juice
6 cups unsweetened grapefruit juice
1 cup real lemon juice
1 -26 ounce bottle vodka

Dissolve the sugar and water over medium heat. Remove from heat and add the juices and vodka. Mix and pour into 2 ice cream pails. Freeze. When ready to serve; fill glass half full of frozen slush and top off with 7-up or gingerale.

In 1974 you did everything you could to look like Marlon Brando or Liz Taylor.
In 2004 you are doing everything you can NOT to look like Marlon Brando or Liz Taylor,

SUMMER BREEZE
(hot summer day + friends + this drink = bliss)

2½ cups ginger ale, chilled
2 cups pineapple sherbet, softened
2 tablespoons lime juice

Place ingredients in a blender and blend until smooth.
Garnish with lime slices and serve immediately.

PARTY PUNCH

1 cup grenadine
1 can frozen strawberry daiquiri
1 can frozen lemonade
1 can frozen pink lemonade
1 can frozen cranberry juice
2 litres of 7-up or lemon-lime soda

Mix all ingredients (except the soda) until dissolved.
When ready to serve, add soda and ice. Garnish with
strawberries or lemon slices.
*Gin or vodka can be added if desired.

HOT SPICED RUM
(Good for whatever ails you)

2 tablespoons brown sugar
1 teaspoon whole allspice
1 teaspoon whole cloves
¼ teaspoon salt
Dash nutmeg
1 cinnamon stick
8 cups apple or pineapple juice (or combination)
1 cup rum

In a large saucepan combine the brown sugar, allspice, cloves, salt, nutmeg, cinnamon and juices. Slowly bring the mixture to boiling. Reduce the heat, cover, and simmer for 2 minutes. Stir in the rum; return just to boiling. Remove from heat; pour through a strainer. Place a pat of butter in each of 8 mugs. Pour in the hot mixture. Serves 8.

It is the weak who are cruel, gentleness can only be expected from the strong. M. Gandhi

STRAWBERRY FREEZE
(This is a variation of the summer slush recipe and can
be used as a base for a delicious summer punch.)

2 packages strawberry Koolaid

2 cups sugar

1 package frozen strawberries

Water added to mixture above to make 6 cups.

6 cups pineapple juice

1 can frozen lemonade concentrate

26 ounces of vodka (optional)

Mix well and put in large container to freeze. (It will
expand so make sure there is extra room.) Freeze,
stirring occasionally.

To serve: Mix ½ slush mixture and ½ Sprite or 7-Up
into a punch bowl or glass.

Make it a great day! The choice is yours.

PINA COLODAS
(It feels like a holiday without going anywhere!)

Lots of Ice
Sweetened condensed milk
Pineapple Juice
Coconut
Rum

Fill your blender with ice and add ½ can of sweetened condensed milk, 4 – 10 ounces of rum (depending on your taste), pineapple juice to fill blender container and a small handful of coconut. Blend until ice is crushed.

ICE RINGS FOR PUNCHES
(These look beautiful floating in the punch bowl and won't water down the punch.)

4 cups sugar free soda (gingerale, orange, 7-up or sprite)
Pour soft drink into mold or bundt pan. Freeze. Pop with no sugar added will freeze harder and last longer. Make a few, freeze, unmold and store in a plastic bag in your freezer!
Optional: Add assorted fruits to decorate such as grapes, cherries, oranges or peaches.

ULTIMATE SASKATCHEWAN WINTER HOT NOG

(Mmmmm... delicious......Nothing beats the winter blues like a steaming mug of this delectable, hot drink.)

½ pound butter
1¾ cups icing sugar
1 cup brown sugar
2 cups vanilla ice cream
½ teaspoon cinnamon
½ teaspoon allspice
1½ ounces of rum per serving
nutmeg and cinnamon sticks to garnish

Let ice cream and butter soften. Mix ice cream, butter, spices and brown and icing sugars in a large pot and cook over low heat until creamy. Store in airtight container in freezer.

To enjoy a serving: Place 1 heaping tablespoon frozen mixture with 1½ ounces rum in a mug and fill with boiling water. Sprinkle with nutmeg and serve with a cinnamon stick.

WASSAILING CIDER
(A great warming drink for outdoor winter activities.)

8 cups apple cider (or apple juice for family caroling)
½ of a 6 ounce can lemonade frozen concentrate
¾ cup firmly packed brown sugar
12 cloves
5 cinnamon sticks
dash nutmeg
Mix cider, lemonade, sugar. Heat covered for 14- 17 minutes. Put spices in a bag and drop into mixture for one hour. Serve warm to cold carolers.

RHUBARB SLUSH
(A very refreshing drink for a hot summer day.)

6 cups rhubarb
⅔ cup sugar
2 cups water
Boil these three ingredients together until mushy- then cool.
Add:
2 cups of vodka or white rum
2- 6 ounce cans of frozen lemonade.
Just before serving add Sprite or 7-Up to taste.

WHITE SANGRIA

½ cup brandy
1 ounce Triple Sec
1 lemon, sliced
lemon juice to taste
1 cluster green seedless grapes
¼ cup sugar
Combine the brandy, Triple Sec, lemon slices,
lemon juice, grapes, and sugar. Measure the
amount of liquid and add white wine in a 3 to 1
ratio. Add ice.

PASSION: A COCKTAIL BEVERAGE

1 ounce rum
2 teaspoons grenadine
6 ounces pineapple juice
Orange slice for garnish
Cherry for garnish
Fill a shaker with ice. Add the rum, grenadine,
and pineapple juice. Shake; pour into brandy
snifter. Top with an orange slice and a cherry.
Serves 1.

In Canada, One in Nine Women
Will Develop Breast Cancer in Her Lifetime.

- The cause of breast cancer is unknown and it cannot be prevented.
- 75% of all breast growths, whether malignant or benign, are discovered during self-breast examination.
- Family history of breast cancer significantly increases one's risk.
- 70% of women diagnosed with breast cancer have no known risk factors.
- Nine out of ten growths are detected by women themselves.
- Eight out of ten breast growths are non-cancerous.
- Increasing age is the second highest risk factor for breast cancer, being female is the highest.
- The highest rate of increase in breast cancer incidence is among women aged 60 years and older.
- Male incidence of breast cancer accounts for 3% of all cases.

Reproduced with the permission of the Breast Cancer Society of Canada, 2004.

Brunches

"Sometimes I've believed as many as six impossible things before breakfast."
Lewis Caroll

BACON AND CHEDDAR STRATA
(Another one of those tasty brunch dishes that you can make the night before.)

12 slices bread, crusts removed and cubed
12 slices crisply cooked bacon, crumbled
½ red pepper, chopped
3 green onions, sliced
4 cups cheddar cheese, grated
6 eggs
3 cups milk
½ teaspoon salt
½ teaspoon dry mustard
¼ teaspoon pepper

Place ½ bread cubes on bottom greased 9 x 13 inch pan. Cover bread with ½ of each: bacon, red pepper, cheese and onion. Repeat layers again. Beat together eggs, milk and seasonings. Pour over bread mixture. Cover and let stand in fridge for 3 hours or overnight before baking. Bake at 350°F. for 45-55 minutes or until knife inserted in the centre comes out clean. Let stand 10 minutes. Nice served with a tray of fruit.

BAKED RASPBERRY FRENCH TOAST WITH VANILLA SAUCE
(A delicious make ahead breakfast.)

1 cup raspberry jam (apricot can be substituted)
10 thick slices bread
2 cups half and half creamilk
½ cup sugar
3 eggs plus 3 additional egg yolks

Butter a 9 x 13 inch baking dish. Spread jam over 1 side of each of the slices of bread. Cut slices in half diagonally forming triangles. Arrange triangles in dish, jam side up and overlapping a bit. Whisk cream, sugar, eggs, and egg yolks in large bowl. Pour custard over bread. Let stand one hour or cover and refrigerate overnight. When ready to bake, preheat oven to 350° F. Bake uncovered until puffed and golden brown, about 50 minutes. Sprinkle with confectioners sugar and serve with vanilla syrup. (great sprinkled with flaked almonds.)
Vanilla syrup: 1½ cups light corn syrup,
2 tablespoons sugar, 1 teaspoon vanilla extract.
Mix ingredients in a small bowl, stirring until sugar dissolves. Let stand 1 hour.

BELGIAN WAFFLES

1 package (2½ teaspoons) yeast
2 cups lukewarm milk
4 eggs, separated
1 teaspoon vanilla
2½ cups flour
1½ teaspoons salt
1 teaspoon sugar
½ cup butter or margarine, melted

Sprinkle yeast over warm milk, stir to dissolve. Beat
egg yolks and add to yeast mixture with vanilla. Add
flour, salt and sugar to liquid ingredients.
Stir in melted butter and combine. Beat egg whites until
stiff and carefully fold into the batter. Let mixture stand
for one hour in a warm place. Cook in waffle iron.

*"A diplomat is a man who always remembers a woman's
birthday and never remembers her age."* Robert Frost

BREAKFAST CREPES
(Takes time, but well worth the effort.)

Batter: 3 cups milk 5 eggs, beaten
½ teaspoon salt 1¼ cups flour
1 teaspoon sugar ⅓ cup butter, melted
1½ teaspoons baking powder

Beat eggs. Add 1 cup milk, salt, sugar and flour. Let sit for about 1 hour. When ready to make crepes, heat remaining milk and melt butter in it. Add to egg mixture along with baking powder. Blend until smooth.

Pour ⅓ cup batter into a 10 inch non-stick frying pan. Fry crepes. Cool on clean counter.

Filling: 2 cups dry cottage cheese
¼ teaspoon salt 2 tablespoons cream
2 tablespoons sugar 2 eggs
1 teaspoon vanilla ½ tablespoon cinnamon
½ - ⅔ cup creamilk

Blend in blender. Add more cream if dry.

Place filling ⅓ way up the crepe in a line.

Use 1 tablespoon filling in each roll, fold ends over and roll up. Layer in casserole dish sprayed with non-stick spray. (Freezes very well at this stage.) Pour enough cream milk over crepes to cover the bottom of the pan. Bake in 350° F. oven for 30-40 minutes. Serve with fresh or frozen strawberries, whipped cream, or maple syrup.

CHEDDAR AND POTATO FRITTATA

(So delicious, you'll think you are in Mexico)

3 tablespoons butter	1 large onion — diced
¼ red pepper, diced	8 large eggs
½ cup cream or milk	1 cup hashbrowns
¾ cup grated cheddar	salt and pepper to taste
½ cup cooked sausage, diced	

Put 2 tablespoons of butter in a frying pan with a metal handle over a low-medium heat. Add onions and sauté, stirring occasionally, for 7 to 10 minutes or until onions are starting to get soft and caramelized. Add red peppers and cook for another 2 to 3 minutes. In a separate pan add the other tablespoon of butter and brown hashbrowns and add crumbled cooked sausage to heat. When potatoes are done sprinkle them over the onions and peppers. Put eggs, cream, and seasonings in a bowl and beat together. Pour egg mixture over onions and potatoes and sprinkle with cheddar cheese. Cook for 10 minutes or until bottom and sides are firm, yet top is still slightly runny. Put the frying pan in the oven under the broiler. Broil for 3 to 5 minutes or until golden brown and set. Cut into wedges and serve with salsa.

BREAKFAST TORTILLAS

(This is a recipe for a large group!)

10 tortillas or homemade soft taco shells

4 tablespoons butter

4 cups hash browns

½ teaspoon salt

¼ teaspoon pepper

4 tablespoons butter

¾ cup green onions, chopped

¾ cup red pepper, chopped

1 ½ - 2 cups Black Forest ham, chopped

8 eggs, beaten

½ cup cream or milk

1 ½ cups cheddar cheese, shredded

In skillet, melt the butter. Add hash browns.
Cook, stirring frequently, until brown and crisp.
Add salt and pepper. Set aside.
In skillet over medium heat, melt 4 tablespoons
butter; cook onion and pepper until tender. Stir
in ham. Beat eggs and cream together. Add to
meat-vegetable mixture; add hashbrowns and stir
until eggs are thickened but still soft.

Continued on next page..................

BREAKFAST TORTILLAS continued...

Microwave wrap for 35 seconds. Place hash brown and egg mixture in center of wrap. Wrap, making sure to tuck in the ends. Place in a casserole. Repeat until all mixture is used. Sprinkle the cheddar cheese over the wraps and heat in 250°F. oven for 20 minutes or until cheese is melted. Serves 10.

"Men weren't really the enemy—they were fellow victims suffering from an outmoded masculine mystique that made them feel unnecessarily inadequate when there were no bears to kill."
Betty Friedan

EASY MAPLE SYRUP

(This is an ideal recipe for maple syrup in an emergency and is just as good as the store variety.)

2 cups white sugar (or brown sugar, firmly packed)
1 cup water
½ teaspoon maple flavoring
¼ cup butter

Heat sugar in a saucepan. Add water and bring to a full boil. Boil for 2 minutes. Remove from heat and stir in flavoring and butter. Store in refrigerator. Makes 1 ½ cups.

You know you are getting up there when you are cautioned to slow down by the doctor instead of the police.

Shown on previous page:

- Breakfast Tortillas...page 38
- Layered Taco Dip...page 13

EGGS POACHED IN WHITE WINE
(It takes about 15 minutes to make
this special breakfast dish.)

1 tablespoon butter
¼ cup dry white wine or vermouth
2 eggs
grated Parmesan cheese
2 English muffin halves (or 2 pieces of toast)
1 teaspoon all-purpose flour
2 tablespoons sour cream
salt and pepper to taste

In a small omelet pan melt butter and add white wine; slip in eggs. Sprinkle grated Parmesan generously over each egg. Cook over low heat until whites are firm (covering the pan speeds up this process.) Lift out eggs onto slices of buttered or toasted English muffins or toast. Add to liquid in the pan: flour, sour cream, white pepper and salt. Stir over moderate heat until sauce bubbles and thickens, about 1 minute. Pour over eggs and serve immediately. Serves 2.

FAVORITE CREAMY CHEESE
FRENCH TOAST
(Goes great with bacon or sausage and fruit plate.)

7 cups white bread, crusts removed cut in one inch cubes
6 ounces cream cheese, cut in small cubes
6 eggs, well beaten
1 cup milk
½ teaspoon cinnamon
⅓ cup maple syrup

Place ½ the bread in greased 8 x 8 inch pan.
Dot cheese on top. Cover with remaining bread.
Combine remaining ingredients and pour over all.
Cover with plastic wrap and refrigerate for a few hours
or overnight. Remove plastic and bake in preheated
375° F. oven for 45 minutes.
Serve immediately with extra maple syrup.

*"Remember, Ginger Rogers did everything Fred Astaire
did, but she did it backwards and in high heels."*
Faith Whittlesey

HASH BROWN QUICHE

1 pound frozen hash browns
⅓ cup butter, melted
1 cup cheddar cheese, shredded
1 cup Swiss cheese, shredded
1 cup ham, diced
4 eggs
½ cup half and half cream
¼ teaspoon salt
¼ teaspoon pepper

Press potatoes into greased 9 x 13 inch pan.
Brush melted butter over potatoes. Bake in
425° F. oven for 10-15 minutes. Remove from
oven. Sprinkle ham and cheeses over crust.
Beat eggs and cream together; add salt and
pepper. Pour over ham and cheese. Bake at
350° F. for 35 minutes or until set.

*"If you don't like something, change it. If
you can't change it, change your attitude."*
                                    Maya Angelou

HOLIDAY HASH BROWNS

1 bag (1 pound 4 ounces) shredded hash brown potatoes
1 medium bell pepper, finely chopped (1 cup)
1 medium onion, finely chopped (½ cup)
2 tablespoons Parmesan cheese, grated
½ teaspoon salt
¼ teaspoon pepper
1 tablespoon butter or margarine, melted
1 tablespoon canola oil
additional grated Parmesan cheese, if desired

Heat oven to 325° F.
Toss potatoes, bell pepper, onion, cheese, salt and pepper. Pour butter and oil into 13 x 9 inch pan. Tilt pan to cover bottom. Spread potato mixture in pan. Bake uncovered about 45 minutes stirring once, until golden brown. Sprinkle with additional cheese before serving.

Make ahead and refrigerate for up to 24 hours before serving.

LUNCHEON MINI-QUICHE

Crust: 12 ounces cream cheese
1 cup margarine
3 cups flour

Mix as pastry and chill for 3 hours.
Roll with rolling pin similar to pie crust, though slightly thinner. Cut with glass to fit in tart tins.

Filling: 3 cups ham, finely chopped
3 cups small broccoli pieces
¼ cup onion, grated
1 cup mozzarella cheese, grated
5 eggs, beaten
2 cups evaporated milk
2 dashes Worcestershire sauce
1 teaspoon mustard powder

Mix all ingredients. Put in shell almost to the top.
Bake for 20 minutes at 350° F.

MACADAMIA NUT WAFFLES

1¾ cups flour
2 teaspoons baking powder
1½ teaspoons salt
3 egg yolks
1 cup whole milk
1 teaspoon vanilla extract
5 tablespoons unsalted butter, melted
3 egg whites
1 -5 ounce can macadamia nuts, finely chopped

Combine flour, baking powder and salt. Add egg yolks and milk; beat with an electric mixer until smooth. Blend in vanilla. Pour in butter, mixing well. In a separate bowl, beat egg whites until stiff and fold gently into batter. Add nuts. Bake in a hot waffle iron.
 Makes 4 – 6 waffles.

"Housewife? A house does not need a wife any more than it needs a husband."
Charlotte Perkins Gilman

MINI SWISS QUICHE

30 frozen sweetened tart shells

Combine next 7 ingredients in blender. Blend
until eggs are mixed in.

10 bacon slices, diced, fried and drained
1 cup Swiss cheese, grated
3 large eggs
2 tablespoons green onion
¾ cup whole milk
¼ teaspoon salt
⅛ teaspoon pepper

Using small container with pouring spout, fill
shells ¾ full. Bake on bottom shelf in 400° F.
oven for about 15 minutes until lightly browned
and set. Makes about 30.

"Of those that say nothing, few are silent."
Thomas Neill

NEVER-FAIL WAFFLES

2 cups flour   1 teaspoon sugar
3 teaspoons baking powder   ½ teaspoon salt
3 eggs, beaten   2 cups milk
½ cup margarine

Mix ingredients in order given and bake in heated waffle iron.

MIDNIGHT FRENCH TOAST

1 dozen eggs   ½ cup cream or milk
1 teaspoon vanilla   2 tablespoons orange juice
1 loaf French bread, sliced 1 inch thick

Mix eggs, cream, vanilla and orange juice in a large container. Add bread, making sure each slice is coated. Cover with a lid and set in fridge over night. Next morning place slices on a well greased cookie sheet and bake 375°F. for 20-25 minutes. Serve with fruit, maple syrup, or whipped cream.

WAKEUP CASSEROLE
(Not even a night owl can sleep through this
wonderful smell coming from the kitchen!)

2 cups seasoned or plain croutons
1 cup cheddar cheese, grated
1 -4 ounce can mushroom pieces, drained
1 ½ pounds fresh breakfast sausage, crumbled
¼ cup onion, chopped
6 eggs
2 cups milk
½ teaspoon salt and ½ teaspoon pepper
½ teaspoon dry mustard
1 -10 ounce can cream of mushroom soup
½ cup milk

Place croutons in greased 13 x 9 x 2 inch pan.
Top with cheese and mushrooms. Brown
sausage and onion. Drain and spread over
cheese. Beat eggs with 2 cups milk and
seasoning; pour over sausage. Cover and
refrigerate overnight. (Maybe frozen at this
point.) Mix soup with ½ cup milk and spread
on top before you bake. Bake in a 325°F.
oven for 60 minutes. Serves 8.

WHOLESOME PANCAKES
(Excellent served with maple syrup,
or fruit and whipped cream.)

1 ½ cups rolled oats
2 cups milk
1 tablespoon baking powder
1 teaspoon salt
½ teaspoon cinnamon
½ cup whole wheat flour
½ cup all purpose flour
1 tablespoon brown sugar
2 eggs, beaten
¼ cup butter, melted

Blend rolled oats and milk, let stand for 5 minutes.
Sift together dry ingredients.
Add dry ingredients, eggs and melted butter to oats.
Pour ¼ cup of batter on hot, lightly greased griddle.
Fry until golden brown.
Turn once.

BUTTERMILK PANCAKES

1 cup flour
1 tablespoon sugar
1 teaspoon baking soda
1 teaspoon baking powder
½ teaspoon salt
1 cup buttermilk
1 egg
¼ cup canola oil

Mix dry ingredients in a bowl. Add buttermilk, egg and oil. Mix well. Spoon onto hot griddle.

In 1974 my husband had long hair - in 2004 he is longing for hair.

Risks of Developing Breast Cancer

Scientific researchers are not certain of the direct causes of breast cancer, but have identified some proven risk factors as well as others that are suspected or possible. You should note that these risk factors increase the chances that you might develop breast cancer, not that you will.

Known Risk Factors:

- Gender: Most breast cancers occur in women
- Age: risk increases as you get older
- Early menstruation (before the age of 12)
- Late menopause (after age 55)
- Having a first baby after age 30 or never having a baby
- Having a close relative with breast cancer
- Being physically inactive
- Being overweight

Possible Risk Factors:

- Eating too few fruits and vegetables
- Drinking too much alcohol
- Never breastfeeding
- Smoking tobacco
- Using birth control pills
- Taking hormone replacement therapy for a long period of time.

Health Canada, November 2002, Reproduced with the permission of the Minister of Public Works and Government Services Canada, 2004.

Breads, Muffins and Loaves

"Nature has no mercy at all. Nature says, 'I'm going to snow. If you have on a bikini and no snowshoes, that's tough. I am going to snow anyway.'"
Maya Angelou

KENTUCKY BISCUITS

(This quick bread is easy to make and excellent
served warm with homemade soup!)

2 cups flour

2 ½ teaspoons baking powder

½ teaspoon baking soda

dash of salt

1 tablespoon sugar

½ cup margarine

¾ cup buttermilk

1 tablespoon butter, melted

Mix flour, baking powder, baking soda, salt and
sugar.
Cut in butter to make coarse crumbs. Add
buttermilk. Mix to make a soft dough. Turn out
onto lightly floured surface. Knead a few times
to make a soft dough (don't over knead). Roll
out to a 6 x 6 inch square. Place on ungreased
baking sheet. With knife, cut dough into 12 even
portions. Do not separate. Brush with melted
butter and dust with flour. Bake at 400° F. for
15 minutes.

LOADED BISCUITS

(We've taken liberty with ordinary biscuits giving them a unique twist...these will complement a homemade soup or stew beautifully.)

2 cups flour

4 teaspoons baking powder

2 tablespoons sugar

1 ¼ cups strong cheddar cheese, grated

3 tablespoons green onions, finely chopped

2 tablespoons green pepper, finely chopped

⅓ cup canola oil

¾ cup cold milk

Mix dry ingredients. Stir well.

Add cheese, onions, and green peppers.

Stir lightly to mix.

Add oil and milk.

Stir to mix, knead.

Pat to ¾ inch thickness.

Cut approximately two inches round.

Arrange on ungreased baking sheet.

Bake at 400° F. for 15 minutes.

THE "BREAST" OATMEAL MINI BREAD LOAVES
(makes 16 mini loaves or 2 regular loaves)

1 cup rolled oats

¼ cup cooking molasses

1 ½ cups hot water

1 egg

3 tablespoons canola oil

⅓ cup brown sugar

1 teaspoon salt

2 cups flour

4 cups flour

¾ cup warm water

1 tablespoon yeast

1 teaspoon sugar

Mix oats, oil, molasses, and egg. Pour hot water over top. Stir. Cool to lukewarm. Dissolve yeast in warm water and sugar mixture. Let stand for 10 minutes. Add to warm rolled oats mixture. Add brown sugar, salt, and 2 cups of flour. Beat well. Work in remaining flour until dough pulls away from the sides of the bowl. Knead until smooth and elastic. Let rise until doubled in size - about 1 to 1½ hours. Divide into 16 equal portions. Shape into loaves. Cover and let rise in the oven with the light on until doubled in size, about 1 hour. Bake at 350° F. for 15 - 20 (45 - 50) minutes. Turn out onto racks to cool.

HARVEST BREAD
(Nutritious and delicious!)

4 cups white flour

1 tablespoon salt

⅓ cup sugar

2 tablespoons fast rising yeast

Mix the above together. Make a well in the center.

Add:

  2 eggs

  ½ cup canola oil

  4 cups quite warm water(not boiling)

Mix well.

Then add: ½ cup ground or whole flax

  ½ cup ground or whole oatmeal

  ½ cup bran or wheat germ

  1 cup whole wheat flour

Add approximately 3 – 3 ½ cups regular flour. Mix well. Let rise in the oven with the light on. Knead down three times, every 15 minutes. On the fourth time, form into loaves (makes four) and put in greased pans. Let rise for another 30 minutes in warm place. Bake at 350° F. for 45 minutes.

MONTEREY BREAD

(This is a nice bread to accompany a soup or pasta, but can also be served as an appetizer!)

1 loaf French bread
1 cup mayonnaise
½ cup onion, chopped
½ cup Parmesan cheese
1 teaspoon Worcestershire sauce
paprika, sprinkle
parsley, sprinkle

Mix mayonnaise, onion, parmesan cheese and Worcestershire sauce together. Slice bread in half-length ways. Butter bread, spread mayonnaise mixture on both halves. Sprinkle more Parmesan cheese, paprika and parsley. Broil till bubbly.

Mid-life means that you become more reflective... You start pondering the "big" questions. What is life? Why am I here? How much Healthy Choice ice cream can I eat before it's no longer a healthy choice?

STRAWBERRY BREAD

3 cups all purpose flour
2 cups sugar
1 tablespoon cinnamon
1 teaspoon baking soda
1 teaspoon salt
3 eggs, well-beaten
1 ¼ cups canola oil
2 10-ounce packages frozen sliced strawberries

Line the bottom of 2 loaf pans with aluminum
foil; lightly grease the pans. In a large mixing
bowl, combine: flour, sugar, cinnamon, baking
soda, and salt. Make a well in the center of this
mixture. Pour the eggs and oil in the well. Stir
until the dry ingredients just become moist. Pour
the thawed strawberries and juice in a container.
With a slotted spoon, dip out the strawberries
and gently stir into the above mixture. Then add
the juice gradually, stirring until the batter is of
the proper consistency. The amount of juice
varies in strawberries when
(continued on the next page)

STRAWBERRY BREAD continued........

thawed, and you do not want the batter to be too thin. Pour into the prepared loaf pans. Bake in a 350°F. oven for 1 hour or until the loaves test done. Let cool in the pans for 15 minutes. With a knife loosen sides of loaves from pans and turn out. Let loaves cool completely before slicing.

GAMES FOR WHEN WE ARE OLDER
1. Sag, You're it.
2. Pin the Toupee on the bald guy.
3. 20 questions shouted into your good ear.
4. Kick the bucket.
5. Red Rover, Red Rover, the nurse says Bend Over.
6. Doc Doc Goose.
7. Simon says something incoherent.
8. Hide and go pee.
9. Spin the Bottle of Mylanta.
10. Musical recliners.

QUICK WHOLE WHEAT BREAD

2 cups whole wheat flour

2 cups all purpose flour

1 tablespoon salt

½ cup sugar

2 tablespoons fast rising yeast

Stir the above ingredients together and make a well. Add:

2 eggs, beaten

½ cup canola oil

4 cups lukewarm water

Mix well. Add an additional:

3 cups whole wheat flour

1 cup all purpose flour

Knead well to make a stiff dough. Punch down every 15 minutes. On the fourth time, form into 4 loaves and place in greased loaf pans. Let rise for 1 hour. Bake at 350°F. for 30 minutes.

PINWHEEL BREAD
(This bread is absolutely beautiful
and it tastes good too!)

1½ tablespoons traditional yeast

2 cups warm water   2 cups milk, scalded

½ cup sugar   ½ cup shortening, melted

2 tablespoons salt   4 cups all-purpose flour

3½ cups all-purpose flour

3½ cups whole wheat flour

¼ cup molasses

Dissolve the yeast in the warm water. Add the
milk, sugar and shortening; beat in the salt and
4 cups of flour until smooth. Cover and let
stand for 1 hour. Stir down and pour half of the
batter into another bowl and add 3½ cups of all
purpose flour or enough to make moderately stiff
dough. Knead 6-8 minutes. To the other ½ of
the batter add the molasses and whole-wheat
flour. Knead 6-8 minutes; cover and let rise for
45 to 60 minutes. Divide each portion into
thirds and roll into rectangles. Place a rectangle
of wheat dough on each rectangle of white dough
and roll up tightly into loaves. Place in greased
loaf pans. Cover and let rise for 45 to 60
minutes. Bake in a 350°F. oven for 45
minutes. Makes 3 loaves.

AWESOME BREADMAKER BUNS
(These are great, light buns. Very good recipe.)

2¼ cups warm water
½ cup canola oil
1 egg
¾ tablespoon salt
¼ cup sugar
6½ cups flour
1 tablespoon bread machine yeast

Throw the first 6 ingredients in your bread-maker. Top with yeast, being careful not to touch the liquid. Put on dough cycle. Later, remove from machine, shape into balls (smaller than tennis ball). Place on greased pans. Let rise until double. (About one hour.) Bake in 325°F. oven for approximately 20 minutes.

"I come from a family where gravy is considered a beverage." Erma Bombeck

GREAT BUNS IN TWO HOURS

2 tablespoons instant yeast
7-8 cups flour (can substitute ⅓ whole wheat flour)
2 eggs
7 tablespoons sugar or honey
6 tablespoons canola oil
1 teaspoon salt
3 cups quite warm water (not boiling)

Mix yeast in 4 cups flour.
In separate bowl whip eggs, sugar, oil, salt and water.
Add flour and yeast mixture.
Blend well and add remaining flour. Mix well.
Let rise for 15 minutes.
Punch down and form into buns.
Place in greased pans, and let rise for one hour.

Bake at 350° F. for 20 minutes.
Makes 4 – 5 dozen.

BUTTERMILK SCONES

3 cups all-purpose flour

⅓ cup sugar

2 ½ teaspoons baking powder

½ teaspoon baking soda

¾ teaspoon salt

¾ cup firm butter or margarine, cut in small

pieces

¾ cup chopped pitted dates, currants or raisins

1 teaspoon orange peel, grated

1 cup buttermilk

1 tablespoon cream or milk (approximately)

¼ teaspoon cinnamon

2 tablespoons sugar

In a large bowl, stir together flour, sugar, baking powder, soda and salt until thoroughly blended. Using a pastry blender or 2 knives, cut butter into flour mixture until it resembles coarse cornmeal. Stir in fruit and orange peel. Make a well in the center of butter-flour mixture; add buttermilk all at once. Stir mixture with a fork until the dough pulls away from the sides of the bowl. With your hands, gather the dough into a

Continued on next page...........

BUTTERMILK SCONES continued......

ball; turn out onto a lightly floured board.
Roll or pat into a ½-inch thick circle. Using a
2 ½ -inch shaped cutter, cut into individual
scones. Place 1 ½ inches apart on lightly
greased baking sheets. Brush tops of scones with
cream; sprinkle lightly with a mixture of the
cinnamon and sugar. Bake in 425° F. oven
for 12 minutes or until the tops are lightly
browned. Serve warm. Makes about 18 scones.

*"Some say the glass is half empty, some say
the glass is half full. I say, are you going to
drink that?"* Lisa Claymen

BUTTERHORNS

½ cup warm water
1 teaspoon sugar
2 tablespoons traditional yeast

Dissolve sugar and yeast in warm water and let set for about 10 minutes.

1 cup sugar
2 cups scalded milk to lukewarm
1 cup margarine
1 teaspoon salt
4 eggs, beaten
6 – 8 cups flour

Mix milk, sugar, melted margarine, salt, eggs with yeast mixture. Add flour, 2 cups at a time until mixture is a smooth dough. Place in greased bowl and refrigerate overnight.
Roll into pie size round and brush with melted margarine. Cut into 8 wedges. Roll from wide to narrow end and brush with more margarine. Let rise for 2 to 3 hours and bake at 350°F. until golden.

Ice with butter icing, and sprinkle with flaked almonds.

MIRACLE OVERNIGHT STICKY BUNS

(A great treat to impress overnight guests, they will think that you stayed up half the night baking!)

1 package frozen dinner rolls (about 20)
1   3 ½ ounce package instant butterscotch pudding
2   cup brown sugar, firmly packed
3   tablespoons cinnamon
½ cup butter, melted
½ cup pecans

Layer in a greased bundt or angel food pan in the following order: frozen rolls, powdered pudding, brown sugar, cinnamon, butter and pecans. Cover the pan with foil topped with a clean towel and allow to sit overnight.
Bake in a 350° F. oven for 30 minutes.
Serves 8 to 10.

MAPLE GROVE EGG BUNS
(You won't find a better recipe!)

2 teaspoons traditional yeast

¼ cup warm water

1 teaspoon sugar

2 cups slightly hotter than lukewarm water

3 eggs, well beaten

½ cup sugar

¾ cup canola oil

¾ teaspoon salt

1 tablespoon baking powder

6½ cups flour (approximately)

Dissolve yeast in water and sugar for 10 minutes and then add remaining ingredients and enough flour to make a soft dough. (Watch your flour after the fourth cup- don't make dough too stiff.) Place the dough in a warm place. Let rise until double in bulk about ¾ hour. Punch down and let rise again. Make the buns the size of golf balls. Place on greased cookie sheets and cover. Let rise in warm place. Bake in 370° F. oven for 25 minutes. This makes about 2 ½ dozen.

MAPLE GROVE CINNAMON BUNS

Make the bun recipe on previous page until you are ready to make into buns. Instead, divide the dough into half, and roll each into a rectangle about 8 x 12 inches. Spread generously with melted butter, sprinkle with brown sugar mixed with cinnamon and 1 tablespoon of flour. Roll up with your hands. Work on the roll to stretch it to about 25 to 30 inches in length and cut the roll in 2 inch thick strips. Place in greased pans (better to use cake pans than cookie sheets). 15 minutes after you put them in pans, turn each bun over and let rise for another hour. Bake at 350° F. for ½ hour or until golden brown. Take out of the oven and tip them upside down. Glaze.

Cinnamon Glaze:

1 tablespoon butter	1 ½ cups brown sugar
½ cup cream	1 teaspoon vanilla

Melt butter in a small frying pan. Add brown sugar to butter and mix well to moisten sugar. Add cream and vanilla. Mix all together and spread on the bottom side of the cinnamon buns.

SCUFFLES

5 cups flour

1 pound margarine

1 cup milk

2 eggs, beaten

2 teaspoons baking powder

1 cup white sugar

2 ½ tablespoons cinnamon

Cut margarine into flour and baking powder; add milk and eggs. Divide dough into 10 balls. Roll each ball as for pie crust and cut into 8 wedges. Instead of using flour to roll out dough, use the mixture of 1 cup sugar and 2 ½ tablespoons cinnamon. Roll the wedges from the wide end to narrow end. Place on greased cookie sheets (or seasoned pizza stone). Bake in 375°F. oven for 20 minutes. Makes a large amount. These freeze very well.

SWEET DOUGH CRESCENTS

2 tablespoons fast rising yeast

½ cup lukewarm water

2 teaspoons sugar

1 cup milk

¾ cup sugar

2 teaspoons salt

¾ cup cold water

½ cup shortening

3 eggs, beaten

7 cups flour

Soak yeast in ½ cup of warm water and 2 teaspoons sugar. Let set for 10 minutes. Add all other ingredients and cover with a towel to rise for 1 hour. Knead down and let rise another hour. Grease baking sheet. Divide dough into 4 or 5 balls. Roll ball of dough with greased rolling pin into circular shape about ¼ inch thick. Cut in 12 pie shaped pieces. Brush with butter, a little brown sugar, and a dash of cinnamon. Roll up beginning at the wide end. Seal point to bun. Place on baking sheet and curve in crescents. Cover with cloth, after top is brushed with butter. Let rise in room temperature for about 1 ½ hours. Bake at 375° F. for 20 minutes. Turn out on wire racks. Cool and ice with white icing. Makes about 4 or 5 dozen rolls.

WHOLE GRAIN BUNS

3 cups warm water
¾ cup sugar
½ cup canola oil
2 eggs
1 teaspoon salt
2 tablespoons instant yeast
1 cup 7 grain cereal
2 cups whole wheat flour
5 cups white flour

Beat water and eggs until frothy. Add sugar and beat. Beat in 2 cups of flour, yeast, salt and rest of liquid ingredients. Add dry ingredients and knead well. Let dough rise about 1 hour or until doubled. Do this 2 times, and form into buns and place on a well-greased pan. Let rise 1 hour and bake at 350° F. for 15 to 20 minutes.

Hint: Make sure your house is draft free and warm. You can use your oven by heating it to 175°F. and turning it off.

BASIC BUN DOUGH
(A nice easy bun dough recipe that makes delicious poppy seed buns)

3 tablespoons yeast	½ cup warm water
1 teaspoon sugar	4 cups lukewarm water
4 eggs	1 cup sugar
1 cup canola oil	1 teaspoon salt
1 teaspoon vinegar	flour, to make soft dough.

Dissolve sugar in ½ cup water. Add yeast and let stand for 10 minutes. Mix together: water, eggs, sugar, oil, salt and vinegar. Add enough flour to make a soft dough. Place dough in a slightly greased bowl, cover and let rise until double in size. Punch down. Let rise again until doubled. Make into buns. Place on greased cookie sheet and let rise. Bake in 350°F. oven for 25 minutes.

POPPYSEED BUNS
Make the basic bun dough. Roll out dough to a rectangle ¼ inch thick and 18 x 12 inch. Spread with prepared poppyseed filling. (filling can be purchased in the bakery department) Roll up and cut into buns, 2-inches long. With scissors snip half way into buns in two places. Let rise and bake in 350°F. oven for 20 minutes. Glaze with icing.

SPICY PUMPKIN LOAF
(Yummy – enjoy with butter.)

1 ½ cups all-purpose flour
1 teaspoon baking powder
1 teaspoon baking soda
½ teaspoon salt
1 teaspoon cinnamon
½ teaspoon nutmeg
½ teaspoon allspice
2 eggs
¾ cup brown sugar
½ cup canola oil
1 cup pumpkin, pureed
½ cup raisins
½ cup nuts, chopped

Mix together: flour, baking powder, baking soda, salt, and spices. Beat eggs, add brown sugar and oil, blend in pumpkin. Add this mixture to dry ingredients. Stir well. Stir in raisins and nuts. Pour into greased 9 x 5 inch loaf pan. Bake at 325° F. for 70 minutes or until inserted toothpick comes out clean. Cool in pan 10 minutes and turn out on wire rack.

APPLE CHEESE BREAD

½ cup margarine

⅔ cup sugar

2 eggs, beaten

1 ½ cups unpeeled apples, grated

1 ½ cups sharp cheddar cheese, grated

½ cup walnuts, chopped

2 cups flour

1½ teaspoons baking powder

½ teaspoon baking soda

½ teaspoon salt

Cream shortening, add sugar, then eggs. Mix well.
Blend in apples, cheese and walnuts. Add sifted dry
ingredients and mix lightly. Pour into greased loaf pan.
Bake at 350° F for about 1 hour.

Make it a great day. The choice is yours.

APRICOT NUT LOAF

(This recipe is very nutritious, a great source of energy for the athletes in your life.)

1 cup all-purpose flour

1 cup whole wheat flour

1 cup raisins

⅔ cup skim milk powder

½ cup brown sugar, packed

½ cup dried apricots, finely chopped

¼ cup almonds or pecans, finely chopped

2 teaspoons baking powder

½ teaspoon baking soda

½ teaspoon salt

3 eggs

¾ cup fresh orange juice

½ cup canola oil

½ cup molasses

2 bananas

In large bowl, combine all-purpose and whole-wheat flours, raisins, skim milk powder, sugar, apricots, pecans, baking powder, baking soda and salt.
In separate bowl or food processor, beat eggs until foamy, beat in orange juice, oil, molasses and bananas
Continued on next page.............

APRICOT LOAF continued.....

until well-mixed. Pour over dry ingredients and stir until just well moistened. Pour into two lightly greased 8 x 4 inch loaf pans. Bake in 325° F. oven for 1 hour or until toothpick inserted in center comes out clean. Let cool in pan on wire rack for 15 minutes. Turn out and let cool completely.

"Love does not consist in gazing at each other but in looking outward together in the same direction."
Antoine de Saint-Exupéry

BANANA LOAF

½ cup butter

1 cup sugar

1 egg

1 cup bananas, mashed

2 teaspoons vanilla

2 cups flour

1 teaspoon baking soda

¼ teaspoon cloves

1 ½ teaspoons cinnamon

½ teaspoon salt

½ cup sour milk

1 cup nuts, chopped (optional)

In large mixing bowl cream together the butter
and sugar; add the egg, bananas and vanilla.
Add the remaining ingredients. Bake in a well-
greased and floured loaf pan in a 350° F. oven
for 1-hour.

Shown on previous page:

Roll Tray
- Maple Grove Cinnamon Buns...page 69
- Basic Bun Dough (Poppyseed Buns)...page 73
- Butterhorns...page 66
- Buttermilk Pancakes...page 51
- Saskatoon Berry Sauce...page 283

CARROT LOAF
(A large recipe — 2 to eat and 2
for the deep freeze.)

4 cups white sugar
3 cups canola oil
8 eggs
6 cups flour
4 teaspoons baking powder
2 teaspoons baking soda
2 teaspoons salt
4 teaspoons cinnamon
2 cups mixed fruit
6 cups carrots, shredded
2 cups dates, chopped
2 - 4 cups raisins
1 cup nuts, chopped (optional)

Beat together sugar and oil. Gradually add
eggs. Stir together: flour, baking powder,
baking soda, salt and cinnamon in a large bowl.
Add to flour: carrots, mixed fruit, dates and
raisins. Stir into the egg mixture. Divide into 4
loaf pans, greased and floured. Bake at 325°
F. for 1 ½ hours.

CHERRY NUT LOAF

2 cups sifted flour

1 cup sugar

3 teaspoons baking powder

½ teaspoon salt

2 eggs

¼ cup milk

3 tablespoons canola oil

¼ teaspoon almond extract

⅓ cup maraschino cherry juice

1 cup maraschino cherries, cut into halves

½ cup walnuts, chopped

Preheat oven to 350°F. Sift four, and mix with sugar, baking powder and salt into a mixing bowl. In a second bowl beat eggs, milk, cherry juice, oil and almond extract. Stir wet into dry ingredients. Beat hard for two minutes or until smooth. Stir in cherries and nuts. Spoon into greased and floured 9 x 5 x 2 inch loaf pan. Bake for 50 minutes.

GLAZED LEMON LOAF
(Delicious- buttered and served with coffee.)

6 tablespoons shortening
1 cup white sugar
2 eggs, well beaten
zest of one lemon, grated
½ cup milk
1 ½ cups flour
¼ teaspoon salt
1 ½ teaspoons baking powder

Preheat oven to 350°F. and line a loaf pan with buttered wax paper. Stir flour, baking powder and salt together in small bowl. Cream shortening and sugar together in larger bowl. Add eggs. Add milk, dry ingredients and lemon rind. Pour batter into prepared loaf pan and bake at 350° F. for 1 hour. Remove from oven. While still warm apply glaze.

Glaze:

½ cup sugar
juice of one lemon
Mix together and spread over the top of the cake until it has absorbed all of the lemon juice.

POPPY SEED LOAF
(This is a tasty treat served with sliced cheese.)

2¼ cups flour

1 cup sugar

¼ cup poppy seed

3½ teaspoons baking powder

1 teaspoon baking soda

1 egg

1¼ cups milk

⅓ cup canola oil

1 teaspoon vanilla

Mix ingredients in order given and pour into about four soup cans for small round loaves or in a loaf pan. Bake for 50 to 55 minutes at 350° F.

"I cannot hear what you say for listening to what you are."　　　*Robert Louis Stevenson*

COTTAGE CHEESE MUFFINS
(These muffins with their low-fat content are considered heart-smart.)

¼ cup butter, melted
1 pound dry curd cottage cheese
3 tablespoons sugar
1 cup flour
2 teaspoons baking powder
1 teaspoon baking soda
½ teaspoon salt
3 eggs

Sift together the flour, sugar, baking powder, baking soda and salt. Stir the cottage cheese into the sifted dry ingredients until all the particles of cheese have been separated. Combine the egg and melted butter and beat well. Add to the dry ingredients in a few swift strokes. Fill well greased muffin tins ⅔'s full and bake at 350°F. for 20 to 25 minutes. Makes 12 muffins.

APPLE STRUESEL OATMEAL MUFFINS

1½ cups hot milk
1½ cups quick cooking rolled oats
1 cup flour
1 tablespoon baking powder
½ teaspoon baking soda
2½ teaspoons cinnamon
1 apple, peeled and chopped
⅔ cup toffee bits
½ cup brown sugar
⅓ cup butter, melted
1 teaspoon vanilla
2 eggs, beaten

Pour hot milk over oats, stir and let stand for 5 minutes. In a separate bowl, mix flour, baking powder, baking soda, cinnamon, apple and toffee bits. In a small bowl beat brown sugar, melted butter, vanilla and eggs. Blend into oatmeal mixture. Pour over dry ingredients and mix until moistened. Fill muffin cups and top with:

Continued on next page.............

APPLE STRUESEL OATMEAL MUFFINS
continued............

1 tablespoons cold butter, diced
4 tablespoons flour
2 tablespoons rolled oats
⅓ cup toffee bits

Cut butter in flour until crumbly. Stir in oats and toffee bits. Bake in 400°F. oven for 18 minutes. Makes 12 large muffins.

"Grow old along with me! The best is yet to be." - Robert Browning

CHOCOLATE CHIP MUFFINS
(A very soft, cake-like muffin)

2 cups flour
1 cup sugar
¾ cup butter
1 teaspoon baking soda
1 egg
½ cup milk chocolate chips
1 cup buttermilk

Mix flour, sugar and butter with a pastry blender until crumbly. Reserve ½ cup for topping. Add the rest of the ingredients individually, mixing well with each one. Line muffin tin with liners. Half fill them with batter. Sprinkle reserved topping on the muffins. Bake in a 375°F. oven for 15-20 minutes. Let sit in the pan for 5 minutes to cool.

You know you are getting old when -
A sexy thing catches your fancy and
your pacemaker opens the garage door.

LEMON CRUNCH BLUEBERRY MUFFINS

1 ¾ cups flour
⅓ cup wheat germ
⅓ cup sugar
3 teaspoons baking powder
½ teaspoon salt
1 cup milk
¼ cup canola oil
1 egg
1 cup blueberries

2 tablespoons sugar
2 tablespoons lemon zest, grated

In bowl combine flour, wheat germ, sugar, baking powder and salt. Stir well. Combine milk, oil and egg in small bowl. Beat well. Add liquid ingredients to dry ingredients. Stir just to moisten. Fold in blueberries. Fill muffin tins ⅔ full. Combine sugar and lemon zest. Sprinkle on muffins before baking. Bake at 425° F. for 20-25 minutes. Makes 1 dozen large muffins.

GLAZED BANANA CHOCOLATE CHIP MUFFINS

3 cups flour
1 tablespoon baking powder
½ teaspoon baking soda
1 ½ cups milk
3 eggs
½ cup butter, melted
¾ cup white sugar
1 teaspoon grated orange peel (optional)
3 ripe bananas, mashed
1 cup chocolate chips
In large bowl, combine flour, baking powder and
soda. Set aside. In bowl beat milk, eggs,
butter, sugar and grated peel. Stir in mashed
bananas. Mix with dry ingredients and stir until
just moistened. Gently fold in chocolate chips.
Fill muffin cups to the top and bake in 375°F.
oven for 15-20 minutes. Remove from heat,
and cool. Glaze: Mix together and boil for 2
minutes: 1 teaspoon grated orange peel,
3 tablespoons orange juice, and ⅓ cup icing
sugar. Brush glaze on top of cooled muffins.

NARAMATA GRAPE MUFFINS

(You have to watch for these grapes to hit the stores in the fall – it is a short season.)

2½ cups flour
1 cup granulated sugar
2½ teaspoons baking powder
¼ teaspoon salt
1 cup buttermilk
1 teaspoon vanilla
2 medium eggs, well beaten
½ cup butter or margarine, melted
1½ cups Okanagan Coronation grapes (seedless)

Preheat oven to 375° F. Line muffin tins with 12 jumbo paper cups. Combine flour, sugar, baking powder and salt. Make a well in the centre. Add buttermilk, eggs, butter and vanilla. Stir until ingredients are just combined. Lightly fold in grapes. Bake 25 minutes or until golden brown on top. Cool in pan.
*You can extend the season of these grapes by freezing them in 1½ cup batches and throwing them into the batter frozen.

PEACH SHORTCAKE MUFFINS

1 ⅔ cups flour
½ cup sugar
2 ½ teaspoons baking powder
¼ teaspoon salt
½ teaspoon ginger
6 tablespoons margarine
1 cup milk
1 ⅔ cups chopped peaches or 1 -19 ounce can sliced peaches

Topping
2 tablespoons sugar
½ teaspoon cinnamon

Muffin: Combine first 5 dry ingredients in large bowl. Cut in margarine with pastry blender until crumbly. Add milk and peaches, stirring just until blended. Spoon into greased muffin cups. Sprinkle with topping mixture. Bake at 400°F. for 20 – 25 minutes, or until set and golden.
Note: You can replace peaches with strawberries if you wish.

SASKATCHEWAN RHUBARB MUFFINS

(One of the greatest joys of spring on the prairies is the first picking of new, young rhubarb. It grows prolifically and is an excellent source of essential nutrients.)

1 cup brown sugar

⅓ cup canola oil

2 eggs

2 teaspoons vanilla

1 teaspoon soda

1 teaspoon baking powder

2 cups rhubarb, chopped

1 cup buttermilk

2 ½ cups flour

½ teaspoon salt

Topping:

4 tablespoons sugar

1 teaspoon cinnamon

Mix dry ingredients.

In large bowl mix sugar, oil, eggs and vanilla.

Add dry ingredients, alternately with buttermilk.

Fold in rhubarb. Put in lightly greased muffin tins.

Sprinkle topping mixture on top. Bake at 400° F. for around 15-20 minutes. Makes 24 muffins.

(Saskatoons are also excellent substituted for the rhubarb).

TANGY CHEESE MUFFINS
(These are a great complement to the Steak Bake with the Entrees!)

1 ¼ cups flour
½ teaspoon salt
1 ½ teaspoons baking powder
¼ teaspoon dry mustard
½ cup (packed) cheese, grated
½ cup milk
2 tablespoons canola oil
1 egg

Combine flour, baking powder, dry mustard, grated cheese and salt. Measure milk in a one cup measure and add oil and egg and beat slightly to blend.
Add liquid to dry ingredients and mix only to blend.
Drop by heaping tablespoons onto hot meat mixture.
Bake uncovered 400°F. 15 – 18 minutes or until done.

"People are usually down on what they are not up to."
Hoyt M. Dobbs

Soups

"Only the pure in heart can make a good soup." Ludwig Van Beethoven

AWESOME CARROT SOUP
(A homemade soup - quick and easy to prepare.)

1 large onion, diced
1 clove of garlic, crushed
2 tablespoons margarine
2 cups chicken stock
3 cups carrots, grated or finely chopped
¼ teaspoon dill
¼ teaspoon marjoram
¼ teaspoon thyme
1 cup cream milk

Cook onion and garlic in butter until clear.
Add chicken soup stock. Bring to a boil.
Add spices and carrots. Cook gently until tender with lid
on pot. Add cream-milk just before serving.

*"It is far better to prepare the child for the path,
than to prepare the path for the child."*

BAKED FRENCH ONION SOUP

(A classic soup that takes a few short cuts for busy
households — and is still delicious.)

2 cans Campbell's onion soup

1 medium onion, chopped

1 teaspoon garlic, crushed

2 tablespoons butter

1⅓ cups croutons — any flavour works

1½ cups mozzarella cheese, shredded

2 teaspoons dill

6 slices bacon, cooked and crumbled

½ cup parmesan cheese

In medium soup pot melt butter, add garlic, onions and
dill, sauté till onions are soft. Add onion soup and 1 ½
cans of water. Bring to a boil and add bacon and
parmesan cheese. Simmer for 10 minutes. Put ⅓ cup
croutons and ¼ mozzarella cheese in bottom of onion
soup bowls and add soup until the bowl is full. Top with
remaining mozzarella cheese to form a crust. Add a
sliver of butter to top and place in oven preset to broil.
Cook until cheese is brown and bubbling. Ready to
serve. Makes 4 servings.

BROCCOLI CHEDDAR CHEESE SOUP

(An easy delicious soup that quickly will become a family favourite.)

2 heads fresh broccoli (to make at least 6 cups)
½ cup onion, finely chopped
2 cups chicken broth
3 tablespoons butter
2 tablespoons flour
1 teaspoon salt
¼ teaspoon pepper
3 cups half and half cream
2 tablespoons powdered chicken bouillon (chicken in a mug has a nice flavour and works well)
1 cup cheddar cheese, grated

Chop broccoli into bite size pieces. In 2 cups of water cook broccoli and onion till soft, approximately 10 minutes. Add broth and powdered chicken bouillon. In a separate saucepan melt butter, add flour, salt and pepper. Stirring constantly, slowly add cream and stir until smooth. Slowly add to cooked broccoli and heat to serving temperature. Spoon into bowls and sprinkle with grated cheddar.

BUTTERNUT SQUASH SOUP

6 cups butternut squash, cubed and peeled
3 ½ cups chicken stock
1 ½ cups onions, chopped
1 bay leaf
½ teaspoon nutmeg
salt and pepper
1 cup plain yogurt

In large saucepan, combine squash, stock, onions and bay leaf. Bring to a boil. Cover and reduce heat to low. Simmer for about 20 minutes or until squash is tender. Remove bay leaf. In blender, puree soup in batches until smooth. Return to pan and reheat if necessary. Season with nutmeg and salt and pepper to taste. (Soup can be cooled and frozen for up to 2 months; thaw and reheat.) To serve, ladle into soup bowls. Swirl 2 tablespoons yogurt into each.
Makes 8 servings, each about ¾ cup.

CLAM CHOWDER
(So easy and delicious.)

2 tablespoons butter
½ cup onion
1 cup hot water
1 cup potatoes, raw-diced
½ cup celery, diced
10 ounce can of baby clams and juice
2 cups milk
½ teaspoon pepper
1 teaspoon salt

Sauté onion and celery. Add water and diced potato. Cook until potato is tender. Add clams and juice, milk salt and pepper. Simmer over low heat for 20 to 25 minutes.   Serves 4.

"The bad news is time flies. The good news is you're the pilot." --Michael Althsuler

COLD WEATHER POTATO SOUP

1 tablespoon butter
1 cup celery, chopped
1 ½ cups green onions (white part and 2 inches of green)
3 cups potatoes, peeled and diced
1 cup carrot, chopped
¾ teaspoon dried thyme
¼ teaspoon black pepper
1 teaspoon dried dill
½ teaspoon salt
4 cups chicken or vegetable broth
1 cup buttermilk

Melt butter in large pot over medium heat. Add onions and celery. Cook and stir for 5 minutes or until vegetables begin to soften. Add broth, potatoes, carrots, thyme, salt and pepper. Bring to a boil. Reduce heat to medium low, cover and simmer for 20 minutes. Working in batches, transfer food to a blender or food processor and puree until smooth. Return to pot, stir in buttermilk and dill. Simmer for a few more minutes.

HAMBURGER VEGETABLE SOUP
(Great for those hungry hockey players or fans!)

1 pound lean ground beef
2 cups potato, diced
2 cups canned tomatoes, chopped
2 carrots, chopped
2 teaspoons salt
¼ cup rice or barley
⅛ teaspoon pepper
6 cups water
½ cup celery, diced
1 medium onion, chopped

Brown beef until no longer pink. Put all ingredients in large pot. Add water and simmer slowly for 1 to 1½ hours.

"Most folks are about as happy as they make up their minds to be."   *Abraham Lincoln*

FIRESIDE CORN CHOWDER
(This is a hearty chowder, rich and creamy.)

2 potatoes
4 – 10 ounce cans chicken broth
2 large onions
12 slices bacon, cut-up
10 tablespoons flour
4 cups hot milk
2 cans kernel corn
2 bay leaves
1 teaspoon thyme
pepper to taste
½ cup cream

Cube potatoes – cook in chicken broth for 10 minutes or until tender. Drain. Save potato water and broth. Cook onion and bacon. Stir in flour – cook 2 minutes. Add milk and reserved broth, corn and liquid. Add seasonings. Boil 10 minutes. Add cream.

You know you are getting up there when
'Getting lucky' means you find your car
in the parking lot.

HEARTY BARLEY BEEF SOUP
(An oldie but a goody.)

1½ pounds round beef steak or beef roast cut into small
pieces
1 cup each: chopped celery, chopped onions
1 clove garlic, minced
8 cups water
4 teaspoons beef bouillon
1 cup tomato sauce
⅔ cup pearl barley
1½ teaspoons dried marjoram
¾ teaspoon dried thyme
½ teaspoon black pepper
⅓ cup fresh parsley, chopped
salt to taste

Brown beef in stock pan sprayed with non-stick spray.
Add vegetables and other ingredients. Reduce heat.
Cover and simmer 1½ hours.

CREAMED GARDEN VEGETABLE SOUP

1 large onion, finely chopped
¾ teaspoon parsley flakes
2 stalks fresh celery, finely chopped
4 cups peas
4 cups carrots, diced
4 cups peeled potatoes, diced
4 cups yellow and/or green beans, cut up
2 teaspoons salt
hot water
4 tablespoons margarine
4 tablespoons flour
1 – 2 cups whipping cream or milk

In Dutch oven, add 2 inches of water. Bring to a boil and add onion. Cook until soft and add parsley and celery. Cook a few minutes and add peas, carrots, potatoes, beans and salt. Add enough water to just cover vegetables. If you want a thinner soup, add a bit more water. Bring to a boil and simmer for an hour, stirring occasionally, with the lid on.

Melt margarine in frying pan on medium heat and add flour and cook until flour turns golden brown.

Continued on next page...............

102

CREAMED GARDEN VEGETABLE SOUP
continued..........

Add this to soup in increments and stir quickly to prevent lumping. Let simmer with lid off for about 10 minutes. This thickens the soup. Turn off heat and let sit for about 10 minutes and add whipping cream or milk for a lighter soup. Stir and serve. This soup freezes well.

Note: You can vary the vegetables, based on what you have on hand. Frozen vegetables can also be used.

"Live in such a way that you would not be ashamed to sell your parrot to the town gossip."

MOM'S FAVOURITE CREAM OF CAULIFLOWER SOUP
(May substitute broccoli pieces for cauliflower.)

¼ cup margarine
¼ cup celery, chopped
1 small onion, finely chopped
⅓ cup flour
4 chicken bouillon cubes, crumbled
3 cups boiling water
1 package (300g./10.6 ounces) frozen cauliflower, thawed or equal amount of fresh cauliflower, partially cooked
2 cups milk or half and half cream
¼ teaspoon nutmeg
¼ teaspoon pepper
¼ teaspoon dill

In large saucepan, melt margarine. Sauté celery and onion 3 – 4 minutes. Stir in flour and cook 1 to 2 minutes. Dissolve bouillon cubes in boiling water. Gradually whisk bouillon into flour mixture; bring to a boil. Simmer over medium heat until slightly thickened; remove from heat.

Continued on next page.......

MOM'S FAVOURITE CREAM OF
CALLIFLOWER SOUP continued...

In a food processor blender, process half of the cauliflower; chop remaining pieces. Add onion, celery and bouillon mixture to puréed cauliflower.
Process until smooth. Return to saucepan with the thickened bouillon mixture; add milk, spices and chopped cauliflower. Reheat to serving temperature. Garnish with grated cheese if desired or stir in 2 tablespoons cheese whiz while reheating

*Note: Processing in blender or food processor is optional.

'Big people talk about ideas; mediocre people talk about things; and little people talk about people."
Tobias S. Gibson

POTATO SOUP IN A HURRY

8 large potatoes, peeled and finely chopped
1 tablespoon onion, chopped
3 tablespoons flour
2 cups half and half cream
1 – 2 tablespoons Chicken soup base
Salt and pepper
Sprinkle parsley

Cook and mash potatoes in usual manner.
(Left-over potatoes also work well.) In stock pot,
place mashed potatoes. Cover with boiling water
to 1-inch above the potatoes. Add chopped
onion, salt and pepper to taste. Stir well. Bring
to a boil and cook for 10 minutes. In a small
bowl take 3 tablespoons flour and enough cream
to make a paste. Continue to add cream for a
smooth consistency, stir well to eliminate any
lumps in the mixture. Slowly pour this mixture
into the soup stirring constantly. Bring it to a
boil, turn the heat down and simmer for about 10
minutes. Continue to stir while adding the
chicken soup base to taste. Cook for 5 – 10
minutes. Before serving sprinkle dried parsley to
give added color.

PRINCESS GREEN BEAN SOUP
(Everyone will want seconds of this soup.)

1 ½ cups fresh green beans (cut in ½-inch
  pieces)
1 medium onion, finely chopped
1 clove garlic, finely chopped
3 tablespoons butter
2 tablespoons flour
2 cups chicken stock
salt and pepper to taste
1 cup whipping cream

Heat butter and sauté beans, onion and garlic,
for 2 minutes. Reduce heat to low and cook 15
minutes. Stir in flour and cook for 2 minutes.
Add broth and simmer for 20 minutes. Add salt
and pepper to taste. Before serving, cover the
bottom of each bowl with cream, pour in soup
and finally swirl more cream on top. Serves 6.

*"Teenager to mother, "Wanting to make the world
a better place to live in" and "cleaning up my
room" are two different things." Leo Garel*

SAUERKRAUT LEAN PORK SOUP

4 cups sauerkraut
8 pork chops trimmed and cubed
1 large onion, chopped fine
1 large bay leaf
2 large potatoes peeled and cubed
2 large carrots, grated
salt and pepper to taste
6 cups of water....adding more if needed

Brown cubed lean pork in a little oil.
Add onions which have been sautéed. Put into a soup
pot. Add sauerkraut, bay leaf and water. Bring to a
boil and boil gently for 20 minutes. Add vegetables, salt
and pepper. Simmer for 40 minutes. Thicken with 2
tablespoons of cornstarch mixed with 1 cup water. Bring
to a boil and simmer for a few more minutes.

**I finally got my head together
and my body fell apart.**

WHOLESOME LENTIL SOUP
(A nourishing tasty soup - even kids ask for seconds!)

1 ½ teaspoons canola oil
1 ¼ cups onions, chopped
1 cup celery, chopped
2 cloves garlic, minced
8 cups chicken broth
1 can (28 ounces) tomatoes, diced
1 -10 ounce can undiluted tomato soup
2 cups brown or green lentils (washed)
2 cups carrots, chopped
2 cups yams or sweet potatoes, peeled and diced
1 ½ teaspoons dried oregano
1 teaspoon ground cumin
1 teaspoon salt
¾ teaspoon ground coriander
½ teaspoon black pepper
⅛ teaspoon nutmeg
2 cups packed fresh spinach, chopped

Sauté onions, celery and garlic in canola oil for 3 – 4
minutes. Add remaining ingredients, except spinach.
Bring to a boil. Reduce heat, cover and simmer for 30
minutes, stirring occasionally. Add spinach and simmer
for 15 more minutes. Serve hot. Better the next day.

Defeating Breast Cancer

- Breast Cancer can be cured if caught on time.
- The odds for a complete recovery from breast cancer are highest (90% +) when the disease is detected early.
- Have a check up with your physician annually and do not be afraid to ask questions.
- 80% of all breast lumps are non-cancerous, but inform your physician of any new findings in your breast. A physician is the only one who can make the proper diagnosis.
- Be knowledgeable about your breasts and the danger that breast cancer can present.
- Examining your own breasts regularly is your greatest weapon in the fight against breast cancer.

Reproduced with the permission of the Breast Cancer Society of Canada, 2004.

Salads

"If you have only one smile in you, give it to the people you love. Don't be surly at home, then go out in the street and start grinning 'Good Morning' at total strangers."
Maya Angelou

ACINIDE PEPI SALAD

2 ½ cups acinide pepi — cook in salted boiling water for about 4 minutes. Drain and rinse in cold water.
2 cans orange sections
1 – 12 ounce can crushed pineapple, drained
1 – 20 ounce can pineapple chunks, drained
3 beaten eggs
1 cup sugar
3 tablespoons cornstarch
1 bag mini marshmallows
1 large tub cool whip

Drain fruit, save 1 ½ cups juice; mix fruit with acinide pepi.
In saucepan, combine juice, sugar, eggs and cornstarch. Cook and stir until mixture begins to thicken. Cool and add fruit and acinide pepi mixture. Cover and refrigerate for 12 –24 hours. Just before serving add cool whip and marshmallows.

* Acinide pepi is a tiny pebble-like pasta made of durum semolina. It makes a delicious fruit salad.

THE "BREAST" SUNKISSED SALAD
WITH PECANS

2 heads Romaine lettuce
1 cup pecan halves, toasted
2 oranges, peeled and sliced
¼ cup vinegar
½ cup sugar or ½ cup Splenda
¾ cup vegetable oil
1 teaspoon salt
¼ small red onion, chopped
1 teaspoon dry mustard
2 tablespoons water

Wash and tear lettuce.
Place lettuce, oranges and pecans in salad bowl.
Combine vinegar, sugar, oil, salt, onion, mustard and water in blender and blend until well mixed. This dressing is best when made ahead and refrigerated to blend flavours. Toss on salad mixings just before you are ready to serve. Serves 10.

CALIFORNIA SALAD

1 cup mayonnaise
¼ cup vinegar
½ cup sugar
1 head romaine lettuce

½ cup milk
1 red onion (optional)
2 tablespoons poppy seed
1 pint strawberries, or more

Chop onion, shred lettuce, combine.
In separate bowl, combine mayonnaise, milk, sugar,
vinegar and poppy seed. Slice strawberries and add to
lettuce. Mix dressing with lettuce just before serving.

BROCOLLI DELIGHT SALAD

10 strips bacon, fried crisp and crumbled
4-5 cups fresh broccoli, including peeled stalks
½ cup raisins
1 cup sunflower seeds
½ cup light mayonnaise

¼ cup red onion, thinly sliced
3 tablespoons sugar
1 tablespoon vinegar

Cut broccoli into pieces. Add bacon, raisins, onion and
seeds. Whisk together sugar, mayonnaise and vinegar.
Pour over broccoli mixture and mix well. Serves 6.

CORN CHIP SALAD

(This is one of the oddest combinations but trust the recipe – It really makes a great salad!)

1 can kidney beans, drained and rinsed
½ red onion, sliced
¾ cup cheddar cheese, grated
1 bag corn chips
1 regular bottle Catalina dressing

Combine ingredients and toss with Catalina dressing. Serve immediately. This salad is not a keeper.

WONDERFUL TUNA SALAD

1 can (12 ounces) water-packed solid white tuna, drained
⅓ cup fat-free plain yogurt
1 can (4 ounces) crushed pineapple, drained
1 celery rib, finely chopped
¼ cup sweet pickle relish
¼ cup chopped pecans
1 teaspoon prepared mustard
⅛ teaspoon ground cinnamon

In a medium bowl, mix tuna, yogurt, pineapple, celery, relish, pecans, mustard and cinnamon. Serves 4.

Variation: Add lettuce to make a tuna lettuce salad.

*This salad makes a fantastic grilled sandwich with crusty bread. Grill the sandwich in a skillet with a little non stick spray.

Shown on previous page:

- Refreshing Lime Pie... page 253
- Polynesian Rice Salad... page 125
- Barbecued Chicken Wings... page 3
- Jerk Pork Skewers... page 18

CREAMY WHEAT SALAD

1 to 2 cups of wheat (you can buy cleaned wheat at some of the supermarkets or ask a farmer friend). Soak wheat overnight and drain. Cover with fresh water and boil until tender, about 1 hour. Drain, rinse and cool. Mix:

8 ounces cream cheese
1 small can drained crushed pineapple
2 tablespoons lemon juice
1 large box vanilla instant pudding
1 large tub of cool whip
Fold in wheat, refrigerate and serve chilled.

CREAMY CUCUMBER SALAD

(Excellent served with hot dishes or a cold meat tray)
3 cups cucumber, peeled and sliced
1 small white onion, thinly sliced
½ cup light miracle whip salad dressing
1 teaspoon white sugar
1 tablespoon evaporated milk or thick cream
1 teaspoon prepared mustard
½ teaspoon celery seed
Put cucumber and onion in bowl. Mix together remaining ingredients. Pour over vegetables and stir gently.

CRUNCHY COLESLAW
(This colorful salad is full of fibre and nutrients.)

3 cups green cabbage, chopped
2 cups red cabbage, chopped
½ cup carrots, shredded
½ cup celery, chopped
1 cup cauliflower, cut in small pieces
2 green onions, chopped
½ apple, chopped
½ cup raisins
2 cheddar cheese slices, cut into small squares
½ cup walnuts, optional

Dressing:
¾ cup light Miracle Whip
2 tablespoons sugar
2 tablespoons evaporated milk or cream
1 teaspoon vinegar

In a large salad bowl, toss all of the above
ingredients together. Coat with dressing.
Serves 8.

FESTIVE BROCCOLI SALAD

Dressing: 2 eggs

1 teaspoon cornstarch

¼ cup wine vinegar

½ cup mayonnaise

½ cup sugar

1 teaspoon dry mustard

¼ cup water

Salad: 4 cups fresh broccoli florets

8 slices bacon, cooked and chopped

2 cups fresh mushrooms, sliced

½ cup slivered almonds, toasted

½ cup sunflower seeds

10 ounce can mandarin oranges (drained)

½ red onion, sliced

¼ cup raisins (optional)

In saucepan, whisk together eggs, sugar, cornstarch and dry mustard. Add vinegar and water. Cook slowly until thickened. Remove from heat, and stir in mayonnaise. Cool. Marinate only broccoli in dressing for several hours. Prior to serving add remaining ingredients and toss well.

GARDEN GREEK SALAD

1 seedless cucumber
5 tomatoes
½ red onion, chopped
1 ½ cups crumbled feta cheese
1 cup black olives

Dressing:
½ cup olive oil
2 tablespoon red wine vinegar
¼ teaspoon salt
¼ teaspoon pepper
2 teaspoons dried oregano leaves

Peel cucumber and cut into ¾ inch chunks. Combine
with tomatoes chopped in similar sized pieces and
chopped onion. Combine dressing ingredients and whisk
until well blended. Pour over vegetables, toss to coat.
Sprinkle with feta cheese and olives.

*"I'm very pleased with each advancing year. It stems back
to when I was forty. I was a bit upset about reaching that
milestone, but an older friend consoled me. 'Don't
complain about growing old - many, many people do not
have that privilege."   Earl Warren*

GREEK PASTA SALAD

1 cup fusilli pasta
¼ cup seedless cucumber, chopped
½ cup green pepper, chopped
6 cherry tomatoes, halved
2 green onions, chopped
½ cup canned chick peas
¼ cup black olives, quartered
1 ounce feta cheese, crumbled

Dressing:
1 tablespoon olive oil
1 tablespoon red wine vinegar
2 teaspoons lemon juice
1 clove garlic, minced
½ teaspoon oregano
salt and pepper

Cook and cool pasta according to package directions.
Add salad ingredients to pasta in large bowl. Whisk
dressing ingredients together and pour over vegetables
and pasta. Refrigerate before serving.

GOURMET SALAD WITH
SWISS AND HOT MUSHROOMS

1 large head lettuce or two small head iceberg lettuce
⅓ cup tarragon vinegar
3 tablespoons dijon mustard
2 clove garlic minced
⅔ cup olive oil
salt and pepper to taste
2 cups Swiss cheese, grated
¾ pound fresh mushrooms
2 tablespoons butter

Set salad plates in freezer for at least 1 hour.
Blend vinegar, mustard, garlic, oil, salt and pepper.
Tear lettuce, and toss with dressing and cheese.
Place on cold salad plates. Sauté the mushrooms and
while hot, spoon over salad. Serve immediately.
Serves 6.

*"The nice thing about living in a small town is that when
I don't know what I am doing, someone else does"*
Unknown

JAPANESE CABBAGE SALAD

½ medium cabbage, shredded
2 green onions, chopped
¼ cup sunflower seeds, toasted
½ cup sliced almonds, toasted
1 package Ichiban noodles broken up

Dressing:
seasoning from Ichiban noodles
½ cup vegetable oil
2 – 4 tablespoons soya sauce
3 tablespoons vinegar
1 tablespoon sugar
1 teaspoon salt
½ teaspoon pepper

Combine cabbage, green onions, toasted
sunflower seeds and almonds. Add broken
Ichiban noodles. Pour dressing over, toss and
serve.

Lord, if you won't make me skinny,
please make all of my friends fat.

KEEPER CUCUMBER SALAD

(Keeps for more then six weeks in refrigerator!)

8 large cucumbers, thinly sliced

1 cup onion, sliced

1 cup celery, diced

1 green pepper, diced

1 sweet red pepper, diced

1 ½ tablespoons pickling salt

Mix together and let stand ½ hour.

2 cups sugar

1 cup white vinegar

1 teaspoon celery seed

Stir until sugar is dissolved (do not boil this mixture) and pour over drained cucumber. Put into jars and keep in refrigerator.

QUICK AND EASY CAESAR SALAD

1 head Romaine lettuce

¼ cup Caesar salad dressing

⅓ cup Ranch salad dressing

2 tablespoons lemon juice

⅛ cup Parmesan cheese

1 cup croutons

¼ cup real bacon bits

Mix salad dressings, lemon juice and cheese and pour over torn lettuce. Toss with croutons and bacon bits.

OVERNIGHT CREAMY FRUIT SALAD
(Give this a try with your turkey suppers and it will become a holiday classic!)

1-14 ounce can pineapple
1 ½ cups chopped walnuts
½ pound mini coloured marshmallows
½ pound seedless grapes cut in half
¼ cup maraschino cherries
1-10 ounce tin mandarin orange segments

Dressing:
6 tablespoons sugar
6 tablespoons pineapple juice
4 tablespoons vinegar
2 egg yolks
¾ cup cream, whipped

Beat first four dressing ingredients together until smooth. Pour into heavy saucepan and over medium heat, bring to a boil. Simmer for 3 to 4 minutes until thick. Cool. Fold in whipped cream. Add the fruit and let stand in refrigerator overnight. Just before serving add 2 sliced bananas. Garnish with more whipped cream, nuts and cherries.

PEACH and ALMOND SALAD

10 ounces spinach, washed and trimmed
8 large mushrooms, sliced
1 cup gruyere cheese, grated
1 cup red seedless grapes
1 ½ cup fresh peach slices
¼ cup almonds, toasted
1 cup mayonnaise
½ cup orange juice concentrate
¼ teaspoon ground cinnamon

Tear spinach into bite size pieces. Add mushrooms, cheese, grapes, peach slices and almonds.

In small mixing bowl; blend together mayonnaise, juice and cinnamon. Just before you are ready to serve toss salad with dressing. Serve on chilled plates.

"If stupidity got us into this mess, why can't it get us out?"   *Will Rogers*

POLYNESIAN RICE SALAD

2 cups cooked rice
1 cup cooked peas, cooled
½ cup celery, chopped
½ cup green peppers, chopped
4 green onions, chopped
1 small can shrimp
1 cup Chinese dry noodles

Dressing
½ cup oil
3 tablespoons soya sauce
¼ teaspoon Accent
½ teaspoon celery seed
1 tablespoon vinegar
½ teaspoon sugar

Put rice and vegetables into a large bowl. Place in refrigerator. Just before serving add a tin of drained shrimp and a cup of Chinese dry noodles. Pour over dressing, toss and serve.

Give me the luxuries of life and I will gladly do without the necessities.

RASPBERRY-PISTACHIO SALAD

1 small bunch romaine, torn into bite size
  pieces (about 10 cups)
1 -7 ounce jar roasted bell peppers, drained and
  cut into ½ inch strips
½ cup raspberries
⅓ cup pistachio nuts, chopped

Toss lettuce, bell peppers, raspberries and nuts. Dress
with champagne vinaigrette.

Champagne vinaigrette dressing:
½ cup champagne vinegar or cider vinegar
¼ cup vegetable oil
1 tablespoon sugar
1 tablespoon Dijon mustard

Prepare champagne vinaigrette. Mix well. Toss with
lettuce, peppers, raspberries and nuts. Serve
immediately.

**If you want your spouse to listen and pay
strict attention to everything you say, talk
in your sleep.**

ROMAINE SALAD WITH
SHERRY VINAIGRETTE

2 tablespoons extra virgin olive oil
3 tablespoons sherry vinegar
1 tablespoon mayonnaise
1 tablespoon lemon juice
1 teaspoon sugar
¼ teaspoon salt
¼ teaspoon ground white or black pepper
1 head romaine lettuce, torn
1 red bell pepper, chopped
½ cup toasted walnuts, chopped
¼ cup crumbled blue cheese

In a small bowl, mix oil, vinegar, mayonnaise, lemon
juice, sugar, salt and white or black pepper.
In a large bowl, combine lettuce, bell pepper, walnuts,
and cheese. Add dressing to salad and toss to coat.
Serves 8.

*"It is not a lack of love, but a lack of friendship that
makes unhappy marriages."*   *Friedrich Nietzsche*

SEISTA ONIONS

(Summer barbecues are not complete without this as a side dish. Simple to prepare and delicious.)

6 large onions, sliced thinly

1 ½ cups vinegar

1 ½ cups water

2 ¼ cups sugar

Bring vinegar, water and sugar to a boil. Cool. Pour over onions. Soak 3 – 5 hrs. Drain onions and discard liquid. To onions add:

1 ½ cups mayonnaise

2 teaspoons celery seed

Mix well and serve. This will keep well in the fridge.

ROTINI-PARMESAN SALAD

½ pound rotini pasta- cooked as per instructions on package and cooled.

2 cups ham, cubed   5 green onion, diced

2 cups broccoli florets   1 cup carrots, chopped

½ cup Italian salad dressing

½ cup parmesan   ½ cup mayonnaise

Toss pasta, ham, onion, broccoli and carrots with Italian dressing and cover and place in the refrigerator for a few hours-better overnight. Just before serving add the mayonnaise and parmesan cheese.

SPRINGTIME LIME SALAD
(Great with poultry!)

1 small package lime jello
1 cup hot water
1 ½ tablespoon lemon juice
2 tablespoon carrot, grated
2 tablespoon celery, chopped
1 tablespoon green onion, finely chopped
1 tablespoon green olives (chopped)
½ cup mayonnaise
½ cup milk
12 ounce carton creamed cottage cheese

Combine: jello, hot water and lemon juice and
refrigerate until partially set. While setting prepare
carrot, celery, green onion and olives.
Combine mayonnaise and milk and add vegetables and
cottage cheese.
Fold mixture into partially set jello and pour into oil
sprayed mold.   Refrigerate until completely set.

"The best and most beautiful things in the world cannot
be seen or even touched. They must be felt with the heart."
Helen Keller

TACO SALAD
(A perfect dish for a luncheon or a light supper.)

1 ¼ pounds lean ground beef, browned and drained
1 package taco seasoning
1 tomato, chopped
1 head lettuce, chopped
1 green pepper, chopped
4 green onions, chopped
1 small can of kidney beans, drained and rinsed
1 ½ cups cheddar cheese, grated
1 package taco chips, crunched
Dressing:
¼ cup taco sauce
1 cup mayonnaise or Miracle Whip
1 tablespoon vinegar
1 tablespoon lemon juice

Add taco seasoning to browned hamburger according to package directions. Allow to cool.
Meanwhile mix all salad ingredients except for taco chips. Add cooled hamburger mixture and toss until mixed. Mix dressing ingredients and toss with salad. Add taco chips just before serving.
* If you are in a hurry Catalina is also a nice dressing for this salad.

TANGY FETA SALAD

½ small head curly endive
½ small head iceberg lettuce
1 small cucumber
4 large tomatoes
8 green or black olives, pitted and halved
1 medium red onion, sliced
½ pound feta cheese
5 tablespoons olive oil
2 tablespoons red wine vinegar
1 teaspoon fresh marjoram or oregano, chopped
½ teaspoon salt
¼ teaspoon black pepper
½ teaspoon prepared mustard

Tear endive and lettuce into bite size pieces and set aside.
Thinly slice cucumber and set aside. Slice tomatoes very
thin. Place endive, lettuce, cucumber, tomatoes, olives
and onion in a serving bowl. Toss together until
thoroughly mixed. Cut cheese into ½ inch cubes.
Scatter over the salad. In a small bowl, place remaining
ingredients and whisk together until thickened. Pour
dressing over salad and serve immediately. Serves 4.

VEGGIE PASTA SALAD

(This recipe is quite large and keeps well
for up to a week in the fridge.)

4 cups raw pasta (any shape)
½ cup Catalina or French salad dressing
2 cups carrots, grated
1 cup cabbage, grated
½ cup green onion, chopped
½ cup celery, chopped
2-6 ounce cans shrimp, drained
1 ½ cup mayonnaise

Cook pasta as directed. Drain. Coat pasta with
dressing and cool. Rinse drained shrimp well in cold
water. Add vegetables, shrimp and mayonnaise.
Let stand at least 12 hours in fridge.

*"Getting a dog is like getting married. It teaches you to be
less self-centered, to accept sudden surprising outbursts of
affection, and not to be upset by a few scratches on
your car."*   *Will Stanton*

Entrees

"Happiness is the only good. The time to be happy is now. The place to be happy is here. The way to be happy is to make others so." *Robert G. Ingersoll*

BEST EVER CHICKEN

5 – 6 chicken breasts
1 ½ cups Swiss cheese, shredded
2 cups fresh mushrooms, sliced
1 can chicken noodle soup
1 package chicken stove top stuffing
¼ cup butter, melted
sprinkle of paprika

Slice chicken breasts and place in a 9x13 inch baking dish. Cover with shredded Swiss cheese and fresh mushrooms. Pour over can of undiluted chicken noodle soup. Cover with a package of stove top stuffing crumbs and seasonings. Drizzle melted butter over top. Sprinkle with paprika. Bake in a 350° F. oven for 1 hour.

The older you get, the tougher it is to lose weight, because by then your body and your fat are really good friends.

THE "BREAST" CHAMPAGNE CHICKEN AND SHRIMP

(The women at our Breast Cancer Banquet loved this chicken and it wasn't too difficult to make enough for 150 women. We had no catering experience. This recipe makes more sauce than you need so, although we did 160 breasts, we only multiplied the sauce recipe by 15.)

20-30 shrimp, (tailed and deveined or precooked shrimp)

2 green onions

2 tablespoons lemon juice

1 teaspoon salt and ½ teaspoon pepper

1 cup water

¼ cup flour

1 cube chicken bouillon

3 tablespoons butter

6 boneless skinless chicken breasts

¾ pound mushrooms, thinly sliced

2 cups heavy cream

1 cup champagne

Shell and devein shrimp or if you are using precooked shrimp-thaw. In a medium bowl combine shrimp, green onions (cut diagonally in pieces 1 inch long), lemon juice and salt; set aside. In small bowl combine water, flour, and bouillon; set aside.

Continued on next page............

CHAMPAGNE CHICKEN continued.......

Add butter to a large skillet and over medium heat, cook chicken breasts until browned and tender (approx. 10 -12 minutes). Add ⅓ cup champagne to the frying pan and simmer the chicken breasts for another 3-4 minutes. While chicken is simmering cook mushrooms in another frying pan, until tender. Remove with slotted spoon when done. Drain shrimp and in the mushroom skillet over high heat cook shrimp mixture until shrimp turns pink about 5 to 7 minutes or 1-2 minutes to heat precooked shrimp. Remove chicken to a platter and keep warm. Stir flour mixture (set aside earlier) into chicken skillet until blended. Gradually add cream and champagne. Cook, stirring constantly until mixture thickens and boils; stir in mushrooms; heat thoroughly. Place a few shrimp on each chicken breast and pour sauce over chicken and shrimp. Dish can be prepared ahead and reheated.

(Because we were doing this for large numbers, we cooked the chicken breasts in late afternoon and put them in a warming oven on trays under foil....we did the sauce and put it into crock pots to stay warm and then added the mushrooms just a few minutes before serving. We cooked the shrimp and when we were making up plates — just added shrimp to the top of each breast-poured over about ⅓ cup of sauce and—rave reviews.)

CHICKEN CACCIATORE

(This is a great meal served with a Ceasar salad and shell shaped pasta.)

⅓ cup all-purpose flour

1 teaspoon salt

¼ teaspoon pepper

3 pounds chicken pieces

¼ cup butter or margarine

1 cup onion, chopped

green pepper, chopped

1 -10 ounce can sliced mushrooms, drained

7 ½ ounce can tomato sauce

14 ounce can tomatoes

1 bay leaf

½ teaspoon oregano

¼ teaspoon garlic powder

1 teaspoon granulated sugar

¼ teaspoon thyme

¼ teaspoon basil

grated parmesan cheese, sprinkle.

Combine flour, salt and pepper in paper or plastic bag. Put 2 or 3 chicken pieces into bag at a time. Shake to coat. Brown in butter in frying pan or large heavy Dutch oven. Remove Continued on next page.............

chicken as it is browned. Add onion and green pepper to pan. Sauté until soft. Add more butter if needed. Measure in next 9 ingredients. Stir. Add chicken. Sprinkle with grated Parmesan cheese. Cover. Simmer slowly for about 35 to 40 minutes until tender. Serves 4 to 5.

"Coffee, Chocolate, Men. Some things are just better rich."

CHICKEN A LA KING IN PASTRY SHELLS

⅓ cup butter

½ pound mushrooms, sliced

¼ cup green pepper, diced

⅓ cup flour

3 cups half and half cream

4 cups cooked chicken, cut into cubes

½ cup pimentos, diced

2 egg yolks

2 tablespoons white wine (optional)

1 teaspoon salt

8 frozen puff pastry shells- baked according to directions.

Sauté mushrooms and green peppers in butter for 5 minutes. Work the flour into the mixture and add the half and half stirring until thickened. Add chicken and pimentos. When it begins to boil reduce heat and cover and simmer for 5 minutes. Beat egg yolks and add a little of the hot sauce from the frying pan to the yolks, then pour warm egg mixture into sauce slowly, stirring until thickened. Stir in wine and salt. Serve in puff pastry shells.

CHICKEN CORDON BLEU

(There are lots of renditions of this recipe —
but this is our all-time favorite!)

6 whole chicken breasts
6 slices Swiss cheese
6 slices cooked ham
4 tablespoons flour
1 teaspoon paprika
3 tablespoons butter or margarine
⅛ cup white wine
2 tablespoons chicken in a mug
1 tablespoon cornstarch
1½ cups heavy cream

Spread chicken breasts flat, enclosing 1 slice cheese and 1
slice ham. Secure edges with toothpicks to seal.
Coat chicken pieces with flour and paprika. In frying
pan brown chicken in butter until brown on all sides, 10
to 15 minutes. Add wine and chicken in a mug and
simmer till tender, about 30 minutes. Remove
toothpicks. Remove chicken and keep warm. In a small
bowl blend cornstarch and cream till smooth. Gradually
add to drippings in frying pan. Cook until sauce thickens
and serve over chicken.

CHICKEN BREASTS WITH TARRAGON CREAM

4 large chicken breasts, skinned and boned
salt and pepper
6 tablespoons butter, divided
3 tablespoons flour
1 ¼ cups chicken stock
1 tablespoon chopped, fresh tarragon or 1 ½ teaspoons dried tarragon
½ cup sour cream
2 tablespoons Gruyere cheese, grated
2 tablespoons Parmesan cheese

Rub chicken with salt and pepper. Melt 4 tablespoons butter. Sauté chicken for 5 – 8 minutes until browned on all sides. Remove from pan with slotted spoon and set aside. Melt remaining butter in skillet. Add chicken stock, flour and tarragon. Heat and bring slowly to a boil stirring continuously. Simmer 2 – 3 minutes. Return chicken to skillet. Reduce heat and simmer for 20-30 minutes until chicken is cooked. Using a slotted

Continued on next page...........

CHICKEN BREASTS WITH TARRAGON CREAM
Continued....................

spoon transfer the cooked chicken breasts to a heated
serving dish. Keep warm.
Stir the sour cream and the Gruyere and the Parmesan
into the sauce and stir over a gentle heat until the cheese
has melted. Pour sauce over chicken.
Sprinkle fresh tarragon or parsley on top.
Serves 1

A women's rule of thumb: if it has tires or
testicles, you know you are going to have a
certain amount of trouble with it.

CHICKEN ELIZABETH
(A royal treat!)

8 ounces cream cheese, softened
½ cup butter
1 teaspoon pepper
1 teaspoon basil
1 teaspoon garlic, minced
1 teaspoon oregano
1 teaspoon thyme
1 teaspoon tarragon
1 teaspoon parsley
4 boneless chicken breasts
12 cherry tomatoes, halved
4 ounces prosciutto ham, paper-thin
¼ cup white wine

Mix cream cheese, butter and herbs. Blend thoroughly. Pound chicken breasts to uniform thickness. Line each breast with 1 ounce of ham, 3 halved tomatoes and ¼ cup of the cheese mixture. Roll up the chicken and place seam side down in a baking pan. Top with a dollop of remaining cheese and sprinkle with white wine generously. Bake in 375°F. oven for 30 minutes. Serves 4.

CHICKEN NICOISE

8 chicken thighs (skin removed)

⅓ cup lemon juice

2 cloves garlic, minced

½ teaspoon dried basil

½ teaspoon thyme

1 bay leaf

4 teaspoons canola oil

4 small onions, quartered

2 cups (½ pound) mushrooms, quartered

1 -19 ounce can tomatoes, drained and chopped

1½ cups frozen green beans

salt and pepper

In a shallow glass dish, sprinkle chicken with lemon juice, garlic, basil, thyme and bay leaf. Let stand 10 minutes. Remove chicken, save marinade. In skillet heat oil over medium high heat. Cook chicken, turning once until golden brown. Remove chicken and set aside. Add onions and mushrooms to skillet. Cook stirring 2 minutes. Add marinade and tomatoes stirring to scrape up brown bits from bottom of pan. Return chicken to pan. Bring to boil, reduce heat, cover and simmer 40 minutes. Uncover increase heat to medium low and add green beans. Cook uncovered, 5 minutes or until beans are tender crisp. Skim off any fat and discard bay leaf. Season to taste.

CHICKEN FLORENTINE

1 pound fresh spinach or 20 ounces frozen
2 tablespoons butter
1 clove garlic, minced
dash basil and a dash marjoram
1 tablespoon flour
½ cup heavy cream

6 chicken breasts, deboned
flour, salt and pepper for dusting chicken
butter for sautéing

3 tablespoons butter
2 tablespoons flour
¾ cup cream
¾ cup chicken stock
salt and pepper to taste
1 cup parmesan cheese, grated

Clean spinach and cook in boiling salted water for about
4 minutes until wilted. (Just drain frozen spinach)
Melt 1 tablespoon butter in a large pan, add garlic, basil
and marjoram. Continued on next page..............

CHICKEN FLORENTINE continued........
Add 1 tablespoon flour to the herbs and mix well.
Add ½ cup heavy cream and add the spinach to the mixture. Cook until thickened and then pour into a 9 x 13 inch pan. Prepare the chicken breasts by dusting them in the seasoned flour. Melt butter in a frying pan and add the chicken breasts. Brown on both sides and lay the browned chicken breasts on top of the bed of spinach. Melt butter in frying pan used to brown the chicken breasts. Add flour and cook the mixture for a few minutes. Add cream and chicken stock and cook until thickened. Season with salt and pepper and pour sauce over chicken breasts. Sprinkle the cup of Parmesan cheese over the chicken just before you place casserole in oven. Bake at 350° F. for 30 minutes or until chicken is cooked and top is golden brown.

*This dish can be made ahead and refrigerated or frozen until needed. Bring to room temperature before placing in the oven.

* Instead of spinach you can use broccoli, or asparagus.

* Milk can be substituted for the cream.

CHICKEN IN ONION AND BUTTERMILK GRAVY
(A good slow cooker recipe)

1 tablespoon canola oil
3 pounds chicken pieces (legs and thighs, skinned)
2 onions, sliced thin
1 carrot, sliced (optional)
1 celery stalk, sliced (optional)
1 teaspoon salt
½ teaspoon cracked black peppercorns
½ teaspoon dried thyme leaves
¼ cup all-purpose flour
1 can condensed chicken broth, undiluted
1 bay leaf
1 ½ cups peas (thawed if frozen)
¾ cup buttermilk

In a skillet, heat oil. Add chicken in batches, brown lightly on all sides. Transfer to slow cooker. Reduce heat to medium; add onions to pan, stirring until softened and just beginning to brown. Add salt, peppercorns, thyme and cook,

Continued on next page ....

146

CHICKEN IN ONION & BUTTERMILK GRAVY
continued..........

stirring for 1 minute. Sprinkle flour over mixture, stir well and cook for 1 minute. Add chicken broth and bay leaf and cook, stirring until mixture thickens. Pour mixture over chicken. (Add carrots and celery, if using.) Cover and cook on low for 6 hours or high for 3 hours until juices run clear when chicken is pierced with a fork. Stir in peas and buttermilk. Cover and cook on high for 20 minutes until peas are cooked. Discard bay leaf.

The only reason I would take up jogging is so that I could hear heavy breathing again. Erma Bombeck

CHICKEN PARMESAN

(This meal is quick and simple to prepare but soon will become a classic for family or company.)

4 chicken breasts, cut in half
½ cup dry bread crumbs
1 egg
½ cup Parmesan cheese
¼ cup canola oil
1 -16 ounce jar spaghetti sauce
1 clove garlic, crushed
1 -8 ounce package Mozzarella cheese
3 cups hot cooked pasta

Combine crumbs and ¼ cup Parmesan cheese in one bowl. Beat egg in a separate bowl. Dip breast in egg and then crumbs. Fry breasts in oil for 5 minutes each side. Combine sauce and garlic, pour into a 9 x 13 inch pan. Add chicken breasts. Cover with foil. Bake at 350° F. for 40 minutes. Place slices of Mozzarella cheese on top and sprinkle with remaining Parmesan cheese. Bake until Mozzarella is bubbling. Serves four.

CHICKEN QUESADILLAS

This makes a great luncheon dish or appetizer!

1 cup cooked chicken, cut into strips

1 tablespoon canola oil

⅓ red pepper

1 medium onion, thinly sliced

¼ cup tomato, diced

1 ½ cups cheddar cheese, grated

4 (8") flour tortillas

salsa (optional)

sour cream (optional)

Cook chicken and cut into strips. Sauté chopped onion and peppers in canola oil until tender, add chicken. Set aside. Wipe the skillet clean and preheat over medium heat. Place one tortilla in skillet. Arrange one half of the cheese on the tortilla. Sprinkle with half of the chopped tomato, add half of the onion, pepper and chicken mixture. Place a second tortilla on top. Cook one side until light brown, approximately 2 to 3 minutes and then by transferring to a plate and flipping it back on the skillet, heat for another minute or two on that side — until tortilla gets crispy and you are sure cheese is melted. Remove from skillet and repeat with next quesadilla . Cut into sections like a pie. Serve immediately. Serve with sour cream and salsa.

CHICKEN STEW

5 cups chicken stock

14 (4 lbs.) chicken thighs, or drumsticks, skinned

1 bunch (7) small carrots, peeled and cut in half diagonally

1 cup peas

4 potatoes, peeled and cut in 1 inch cubes

2 cups pearl onions, peeled

3 tablespoons butter

3 stalks celery, chopped

1 onion, chopped

8 ounces button mushrooms

⅓ cup flour

1 teaspoon thyme

½ teaspoon each salt and pepper

¼ cup whipping cream

Bring stock to boil. Add chicken, cover and simmer over medium-low heat for 30 minutes. Transfer chicken to plate; let cool. Cut chicken into bit size chunks. Add carrots and potatoes to stock; cover and cook for 10 minutes. Add pearl onions; simmer, covered until onions are tender (5 minutes). Transfer veggies to plate.
Continued on next page............

CHICKEN STEW continued.............

Pour stock into large measuring cup, adding more stock if necessary to make 5 cups. In same pan, melt butter over medium-high heat, cook celery, onion and mushrooms stirring often until softened (8 minutes). Add flour, thyme, salt and pepper, cook stirring for 1 min. Gradually whisk in reserved stock; bring to boil, stirring often for (5 minutes). Return chicken and pan juices. Add carrot mixture, peas and cream, stirring to combine. Drop in dumplings, cover and cook without lifting lid for 15 minutes.

DUMPLINGS:
2 cups pastry flour
1 tablespoons fresh parsley, chopped
4 teaspoons baking powder
½ teaspoon salt
2 tablespoons butter
¾ cup milk (approximately)

Mix ingredients, only until combined.
Drop into simmering stew with a tablespoon.
Cover container tightly. Cook on low to medium heat for 12 to 15 minutes. Serve at once.

CHICKEN TORTILLAS

1 pound skinless boneless chicken breasts

½ cup onion

2 to 3 tablespoons flour

¼ teaspoon dry oregano

1 cup chicken broth

1 -4 ounce can green chilies, diced

3 -7 inch tortillas

3 tablespoons cheddar cheese, grated

1 ounce can green chili sauce (optional)

Brown chicken pieces, cool and dice. Sauté onion until translucent. Put chicken back into skillet- add the flour, stirring till flour disappears. Add oregano and chicken broth to mixture and simmer until it thickens. Cook 1-2 minutes, then add diced green chilies. Warm mixture thoroughly. Warm tortillas in microwave and put chicken mixture in and fold tortilla seam side down. Repeat with remaining tortillas. Place tortillas in a casserole dish and sprinkle grated cheese on top. Chili sauce can be sprinkled on top with cheese. Bake in a 350 ° F. oven for 10-15 minutes until cheese melts and tortillas are heated thoroughly.

Shown on previous page:

- Breast Crab Rolls...page 4
- Breast Hot Mushroom Tarts...page 9
- Breast Oatmeal Mini Loaves...page 55
- Breast Sunkissed Salad...page 112
- Breast Champagne Chicken and Shrimp...page 134
- Breast Rice Pilaf...page 214
- Breast Cheesecake...page 247

LEMON BASIL CHICKEN BREASTS ON THE BARBEQUE
(This is delicious with a tossed salad and rice pilaf.)

4 chicken breast portions or 2 complete breasts, cut in half

¼ cup canola oil

¼ cup lemon juice (fresh is the best)

2 tablespoons white wine vinegar

1 clove garlic or 1 tablespoon minced

1 tablespoon fresh or dried basil, chopped

½ teaspoon salt

¼ teaspoon pepper

Combine all ingredients to make marinade and put in a ziplock bag with the chicken in refrigerator for 1 hour. Brush grill with oil and preheat barbecue to medium high. Cook chicken for 5 to 8 minutes each side or until done.

In 1974 I enjoyed going to a new, hip joint!
In 2004 I'll be receiving a new hip joint!

LEMON CHICKEN

⅓ cup flour
1 teaspoon salt
1 teaspoon paprika
3 tablespoons lemon juice
3 tablespoons canola oil
¾ cup chicken stock
¼ cup green onions, sliced
2 tablespoons brown sugar
1 frying chicken, cut up

In a bag combine flour, salt, and paprika. Brush
chicken with lemon juice. Put pieces of chicken in flour
mixture. Shake well. Brown in hot oil. Drain off fat.
Pour chicken stock over chicken. Stir in onion, brown
sugar and any remaining lemon juice. Cover, reduce
heat. Simmer chicken in sauce mixture until tender, 40
– 45 minutes.

LEMON FRIED CHICKEN
(This dish will become a family favorite.)

2 chickens, cut up
1 cup flour
1 ½ tablespoons salt
dash pepper
1 cup margarine
¾ pound fresh mushrooms, sliced
1 lemon, sliced paper thin
½ cup sherry

Preheat oven to 350° F.
Wash pieces of chicken and pat dry. Combine flour, salt and pepper. Dredge chicken in flour mixture, coating well. Melt margarine in a large frying pan. Brown pieces of chicken on both sides. Remove and place pieces in a large casserole. To remaining margarine in the frying pan add; mushrooms, lemon slices, and sherry. Cook until thickened. Pour over chicken and cover casserole dish. Bake in a 325° F. oven for 1 hour.

MUSHROOM PARMESAN CHICKEN

½ cup bread crumbs
½ cup parmesan cheese
½ teaspoon oregano
garlic powder, to taste
pepper, to taste
4 chicken breasts, deboned
2 -10 ounce cans cream of chicken or mushroom soup
1 cup milk
1 -10 ounce can whole mushrooms

Combine bread crumbs, parmesan cheese, oregano, garlic powder and pepper. Roll chicken in mixture, place in shallow baking pan. Bake 400° F. for 20 min. Turn chicken, bake 20 minutes more. Combine the rest of the ingredients and after 20 minutes pour over chicken. Sprinkle with additional parmesan cheese. Bake 20 minutes more, or until chicken is tender.

QUICK CHICKEN AND RICE DINNER

2-3 pounds chicken pieces, cut up
½ cup ketchup
¼ cup water
¼ cup brown sugar, packed
1 envelope dry onion soup mix
Arrange chicken pieces in roaster or casserole
sprayed with non-stick coating. In small bowl,
combine ketchup, water, sugar and soup mix.
Spread over chicken, making sure each piece is
covered. Bake at 350° F. for 1hour.

2 cups rice
4 tablespoons soya sauce
1 -10 ounce can mushroom stems and pieces
¼ cup oil
1 envelope dry onion soup mix
3½ cups water
Spray another casserole dish with non-stick
coating. Combine rice, soya sauce, mushrooms,
oil, onion soup mix and water. Stir. Bake for
1-hour at 350° F. with the chicken.

SCREWDRIVER CHICKEN

flour

salt & pepper

paprika

6 chicken breasts

¼ cup canola oil

2 cloves garlic

3 tablespoons butter

¾ cup orange juice

¾ cup vodka

dash cayenne pepper

parsley

In a plastic bag combine flour with salt, pepper, and enough paprika to slightly color the flour pink. Add the chicken breasts to the flour and toss to coat completely. Put oil, butter and garlic in a 10-inch skillet or frying pan and heat until hot. Add the chicken and cook until browned on both sides, approximately 3 to 5 minutes. Remove the chicken to a platter and drain oil. Reduce the heat and add orange juice, vodka, parsley and cayenne pepper to pan and stir to scrape up the pan drippings. You may sprinkle some flour in the pan and stir to thicken the gravy. Immediately add the chicken, return the heat to high and cook for 1 more minute. Serves 6.

SOUTHWESTERN GRILLED CHICKEN BREASTS

4 boneless skinless chicken breasts
1 cup of Italian salad dressing
⅓ cup chunky salsa
4 slices of Monteray Jack cheese (or mozzarella in a pinch)

Pour Italian dressing into a ziplock bag with the chicken and allow to marinate in refrigerator for 3 to 4 hours. Brush grill with oil and preheat barbecue to medium high. Cook chicken 5 to 8 minutes on each side or until done. Remove chicken from grill and place in a shallow pan. Spoon a generous helping of salsa on each breast and cover with a slice of cheese. Put the pan back onto the grill (otherwise this will make a mess of your grill) for a few minutes until the cheese has melted the salsa onto the chicken breast.

If I had to live my life over again, I would make the same mistakes, only sooner.   *Tallulah Bankhead*

SUPER SALSA CHICKEN

1 teaspoon canola oil
1 pound (or more) boneless, skinless chicken breasts, cut
in strips
¼ cup onion, chopped
¾ cup medium salsa
⅓ cup light peanut butter
1 ½ cups evaporated milk
1 teaspoon cornstarch
salt and pepper

In large non-stick frying pan heat oil over medium heat.
Add chicken and onions to pan.
Cook and stir until chicken is browned on all sides.
Stir in salsa and peanut butter.
Combine evaporated milk and cornstarch.
Gradually stir into pan.
Cook and stir over medium heat until sauce boils and
thickens. Add salt and pepper to taste.
Great served over rice.

WESTERN MANDARIN CHICKEN

1 -10 ounce can mandarin orange pieces
1 tablespoon soya sauce
1 tablespoon honey
½ teaspoon garlic powder
2 skinless, boneless chicken breasts

Drain the can of oranges and combine juice from oranges, soya sauce, honey and garlic in shallow pan. Add chicken and bake uncovered for 30 minutes at 350° F. Turn chicken and cook 20 minutes longer, basting often. Add orange segments during last 5 minutes of cooking. Serve with steamed rice.

"The heyday of women's life is the shady side of fifty."
Elizabeth Stanton

CHOP SUEY

2 pounds ground beef
1 cup onion, chopped
2 cups celery, chopped
2 cans mushrooms stems and pieces (save juice)
1 tablespoon butter
1 can bean sprouts (save juice)
5 cups cabbage, finely chopped
1 can consommé
1 can juice from mushrooms and bean sprouts
4 tablespoons soya sauce
salt and pepper
3 tablespoons sugar

In a Dutch oven fry hamburger and onion. Add celery, mushrooms, butter, bean sprouts and cabbage. Cook this until cabbage is soft. Add consommé, saved juice from mushrooms and bean sprouts, soya sauce, salt, pepper, and sugar. Simmer for ½ hour. May be thickened with 2 tablespoons cornstarch mixed with ⅓ cup cold water. Stir slowly into the mixture in Dutch oven and simmer until the mixture has thickened.

HAMBURGER PIZZA BAKE

1 pound ground beef
½ cup green pepper, chopped
4 tablespoons onion, chopped
½ teaspoon dried oregano
1 -16 ounce can tomato sauce
1 cup water
1 cup macaroni, cooked
½ cup parmesan or cheddar cheese, grated

Brown ground beef, pour off excess fat.
Add green pepper, onion, oregano, dash of pepper.
Stir in tomato sauce and water. Simmer 5 minutes.
Cook and drain macaroni and mix with above. Add 4
tablespoons cheese. Turn into 1 ½ quart casserole.
Sprinkle with remaining cheese. Cover and bake at
350° F. for 25 minutes. Serves 4.

*"I have everything I had twenty years ago, it is all just a
little lower."*   *Gypsy Rose Lee*

MILD AND SWEET CHILI
(This is a delicious, must try dish.)

2 pounds hamburger
1 onion, chopped
½ cup celery, chopped
1 green pepper, chopped
2 teaspoons salt
½ cup ketchup
1 teaspoon pepper
1 -28 ounce can tomatoes
1 -14 ounce can tomato sauce
2 cans kidney beans
2 tablespoons dry mustard
½ teaspoon cinnamon
1 teaspoon chili powder
½ cup brown sugar
⅓ cup white sugar
½ cup barbecue sauce
1 can mushroom stems and pieces

Brown hamburger with onions, celery and green pepper.
Add all other ingredients.
Simmer for 2 hours.

NUTRICIOUS MEATLOAF

(This is an ideal way to add some hidden vegetables to the kids diet, and it will become a favorite.)

1 ½ pounds lean ground beef

1 cup raw carrots, grated

1 cup raw potato, grated

1 tablespoon dry onion soup mix

¼ cup ketchup

½ cup dry bread crumbs

1 egg

1 teaspoon salt and ½ teaspoon pepper

Mix all ingredients and press into a loaf pan.

Bake for 1 hour at 350° F.

* 1 cup of grated cheddar cheese can be added to the mixture and some additional ketchup brushed on the top.

*Some like a sauce on top of the meatloaf. This adds a little variety.

Sauce

3 tablespoons brown sugar

½ cup ketchup

½ teaspoon nutmeg

1 teaspoon dry mustard

Mix well and pour on top of meatloaf before cooking.

SHEPERD'S PIE
WITH GARLIC MASHED POTATOES

1½ pounds lean ground beef

1 cup onion, chopped

2 cloves garlic, crushed

¼ cup flour

½ teaspoon savory and ½ teaspoon thyme

1 bay leaf and salt and pepper to taste

1 -10 oz can beef broth mixed with ½ can water

2 teaspoons Worcestershire sauce

½ cup carrots, finely chopped

½ cup corn

Brown beef. Sauté onion and garlic. Stir in flour and seasonings. Add broth, water, Worcestershire sauce, carrots, corn and beef. Simmer for 20 minutes.

GARLIC MASHED POTATOES

6 medium potatoes

6 cloves garlic

¾ cup heavy cream

salt and pepper to taste

Cook potatoes and garlic. Mash and add cream. Place meat mixture in the bottom of a 2 quart baking dish. Spread mashed potatoes on top. Cover with foil and bake for 20 minutes at 325° F. Uncover and bake for 10 minutes more.

SHIPWRECK CASSEROLE

2 onions
3 medium potatoes
1 pound hamburger
½ cup uncooked rice
1 cup celery, chopped
1 tin tomato or cream of chicken soup

Slice onions in bottom of baking dish. Add thinly sliced potatoes. Over potatoes spread a layer of hamburger. Next add uncooked rice. Top with layer of chopped celery. As each layer is added, season with salt and pepper. Combine soup with equal amount of water and pour over all. Cover and bake for 2 hours at 350°F.

Whoever thought up the word 'mammogram'? Every time I hear it I think I am supposed to put my breast in an envelope and mail it to someone.

SICILIAN MEAT ROLL

2 eggs, beaten

½ cup tomato juice

¾ cup soft bread crumbs

2 tablespoons parsley, snipped

½ teaspoon dried oregano

¼ teaspoon salt and ¼ teaspoon pepper

1 clove garlic, minced

2 pounds ground beef

4 to 6 ounces ham, thinly sliced

6 ounces mozzarella cheese, sliced

In a bowl combine the eggs and tomato juice. Stir in the bread crumbs, parsley, oregano, salt, pepper and garlic. Add ground beef. Mix well. On waxed paper pat meat to a 10 x 8 inch rectangle. Arrange ham slices on top meat leaving a small margin around edges. Reserve 1 slice of cheese. Tear up remaining cheese and sprinkle over ham. Starting from short end, roll up meat using paper to lift. Seal edges and ends. Place roll, seam side down in a 13 x 9 x 2 inch pan. Bake at 350° F. for about 1¼ hours. Centre will be pink due to ham. Cut reserved cheese slice into 4 triangles and overlap on top of meat. Return to oven until cheese melts (2 minutes). Makes 8 servings.

SOFT TACOS SHELLS

(These shells are so easy to make and so delicious that you will use them for all your tortilla recipes.)

1½ cups flour
½ teaspoon salt
3 eggs
1¾ cups milk

Mix ingredients and let stand 1 hour. Pour about ½ cup dough into a 9 inch frying pan, tilt pan until batter reaches the sides. When light brown, flip and brown other side. Makes about 6 to 8 taco shells.

Filling: Set out dishes of hamburger that has been browned in taco seasoning; sliced chicken breast also browned and spiced; shredded lettuce, diced tomatoes, diced green onion and grated cheese. Serve with sour cream and taco sauce. This makes a great help yourself buffet supper that every age seems to enjoy.

"I have a great diet! You are allowed to eat anything you want, but you must eat it with naked fat people." Ed Blue

VERSATILE MEATBALLS
WITH DILL OR SWEET AND SOUR SAUCE

1 pound lean ground beef
1 egg
¼ cup milk
½ cup bread crumbs
1 small onion, finely chopped
1 tablespoon barbecue sauce
¼ teaspoon garlic powder or minced garlic
salt and pepper to taste
Mix together and form into balls. Brown meatballs and place in a casserole dish. Cover with sweet and sour sauce or mushroom dill sauce and bake at 350° F. until hot.

Mushroom Dill Sauce
2 tablespoons butter
½ cup mushrooms, sliced
1 small onion, finely chopped
1 teaspoon dried dill
1 can cream of mushroom soup
⅔ cup water
Fry onions and dill in butter and add mushrooms, stir in soup and water.

Sweet and sour sauce continued on next page..........

Sweet and Sour Sauce

½ cup brown sugar

¼ teaspoon ginger

½ teaspoon garlic powder

½ teaspoon onion powder or ⅛ cup onion, finely grated

1 small tin pineapple tidbits with juice

1 tin whole mushrooms with juice

2 tablespoons cornstarch

Combine all ingredients and simmer over medium heat until sugar has dissolved. Dissolve cornstarch in a small amount of cold water and add to sauce. Simmer until it thickens.

Did you know that the woman that was considered the most beautiful of all time, Marilyn Monroe, wore a size 14?

171

BAKED HAM WITH MARINADE

6 pound ham — bone removed
½ cup wine vinegar
¼ cup fruit juice
¼ cup brown sugar
1 tablespoon Worcestershire sauce
½ teaspoon pepper
¼ teaspoon cloves
1 teaspoon dry mustard
1 teaspoon ginger
whole cloves

Mix above ingredients except for ham, and heat in a saucepan over medium heat until blended. Remove rind from ham, score the fat and stud with whole cloves. Pour marinade over ham and let sit in the refrigerator overnight. Guidelines: for a six pound boneless ham, bake in covered roaster at 325° F. for about 2½ hours.

GLAZED BARBEQUE HAM STEAK
(A summer favorite.)

4 ham steaks -1 ½ inches thick

2 cups brown sugar

⅔ cup lemon juice

½ cup horseradish

Score ham steaks on both sides ½ inch deep. Set aside.
In saucepan heat sugar, lemon juice and horseradish to
a boil.
On barbecue, over low to medium heat, cook steaks
basting with sauce and turning often until cooked, about
30 minutes.

*If you keep doing what you are doing, you will
keep getting what you are getting.*

JAMBALAYA

1 cup uncooked long grain rice
1 tablespoon dried onion flakes
1 tablespoon dried green chili pepper flakes
1 tablespoon dried parsley flakes
2 teaspoons beef bouillon granules
1 teaspoon chives
1 teaspoon dried celery flakes
½ teaspoon black pepper
¼ teaspoon garlic powder
¼ teaspoon thyme
¼ teaspoon ground red pepper
2 cups water
1-8 ounce can tomato sauce
1 pound smoked sausage, sliced
1 cup ham, chopped

Combine the rice with water, tomato sauce, bouillon and spices in a Dutch oven. Bring to a boil. Cover, reduce heat and simmer 20 minutes. Stir sausage and ham. Heat thoroughly.

SWEET BARBECUED HAM STEAKS

Cut ham steaks ½ to ¾ inches thick.
Place on grill and sear each side.
Brush with sweet barbecue sauce and turn.
Repeat until meat is heated through and nicely glazed.

SWEET BAR.B.Q. SAUCE

2 tablespoons dry mustard
⅓ cup chili sauce
1 cup brown sugar
¾ cup pineapple juice
1 teaspoon lemon juice

Combine and brush over ham steaks.

"I refuse to think of them as chin hairs, they are stray eyebrows." Janette Barber

FETTUCCINE WITH TWO CHEESES AND CREAM

3 cups cooked fettuccine noodles or homemade
    egg noodles
½ cup butter, melted
½ cup heavy cream
½ cup mozzarella cheese, shredded
1 teaspoon fresh parsley, finely chopped
¼ cup Parmesan cheese, grated

Arrange the fettuccine on 4 plates. Combine butter, cream and mozzarella cheese. Cook over low heat until the cheese melts and the cream bubbles and thickens. Add the parsley, stir and pour over the noodles. Sprinkle with Parmesan cheese and serve promptly. Serves 4.

You know you are suffering from PMS when you are counting down the days until menopause

FRESH TOMATO LASAGNA

8 lasagna noodles, cooked
2 cups mozzarella cheese
8 large fresh tomatoes, chopped
1 teaspoon oregano
½ teaspoon garlic powder
1½ teaspoons salt
½ teaspoon pepper

Mix tomatoes and spices together and layer in shallow casserole dish alternately with noodles and cheese. Bake 450° F. for 10 to 15 minutes.

"I have yet to hear a man ask for advice on how to combine marriage and a career."

LASAGNA

(This is a time-consuming recipe, but a delicious lasagna. It makes 2 -9 x 13 inch pans. Bake one and freeze one for another day.)

1- 2 onions	2 pounds ground beef
2 cans mushrooms	2 celery stalks
2 large carrots	1 green pepper
2 large cans tomatoes	1 teaspoon baking soda
1 teaspoon sugar	3- 4 bay leaves

2 small cans tomato paste
1 teaspoon salt
1 teaspoon pepper
garlic salt, celery salt, and onion salt, to taste
4 pounds mozzarella cheese, shredded
2 pounds dry curd cottage or 1 pound ricotta cheese
2 eggs
Parmesan cheese, grated
12- 16 lasagna noodles, boiled

Brown the ground beef, drain off the excess fat. Add the onion and continue to brown until onion is transparent. Add mushrooms and set aside. Dice celery, carrots, green pepper and put in a sauce pan covered with a little water and boil together until

Lasagna continued on next page............

178

LASAGNA continued.............

partially cooked. Set aside. Bring the canned tomatoes and tomato paste to a boil in a large pot. Add baking soda, salt, sugar, pepper, bay leaves while stirring the boiling tomato mixture. Allow mixture to simmer 5 minutes. Remove bay leaves and add the ground beef mixture. Drain the vegetables and add them to the sauce as well. Simmer together 2 hours stirring occasionally. Season to taste with garlic salt, celery salt, onion salt, salt and pepper. Prepare 2 lasagna pans or 9 x 13 inch pans. Spread ¼ meat and tomato sauce recipe in the bottom of each pan. Arrange 3-4 lasagna noodles on top of meat in each pan . Sprinkle each with (1 pound) shredded mozzarella cheese. Mix together egg and cottage or ricotta cheese. Spread ½ this mixture on each pan over mozzarella cheese. Arrange lasagna noodles on top to cover. Half the remainder of tomato-meat sauce goes on top of each pan. Sprinkle with remainder of mozzarella cheese (1 pound each). Sprinkle with grated parmesan cheese. Bake at 325° F. for 1 hour and 15 minutes or freeze unbaked.

Age doesn't always bring wisdom. Sometimes age comes alone.

NUMBER ONE SPAGHETTI SAUCE

2 pounds lean ground beef
1 -10 ounce can tomato soup
salt and pepper to taste
12 ounces tomato paste
10 ounces tomato juice
¼ cup parmesan cheese
½ cup sugar
3 small red peppers, chopped
2 teaspoons parsley
½ teaspoon oregano, poultry seasoning, sage, nutmeg, thyme
1 cup celery, chopped
1 large onion, chopped
¼ teaspoon garlic powder

Mix all ingredients, except beef, and simmer for one hour. Brown ground beef, add salt and pepper to taste. Add beef mixture to sauce and continue to simmer for another hour. Serve over spaghetti or linguini.

"Have you ever noticed that nothing is impossible for those that don't have to do it?" Unknown

PENNE PRIMAVERA WITH HERB CREAM SAUCE

6 cups Penne pasta
2 carrots, sliced
4 cups broccoli florets
1 tablespoon butter
1 small onion, chopped
1 clove garlic, minced
1 can kernel corn
1 cup chicken stock
1 cup cream
½ teaspoon salt
¼ teaspoon each nutmeg and pepper
½ cup Parmesan cheese, grated
⅓ cup fresh basil, chopped
2 tablespoons chives, chopped

In a large pot of boiling salted water, cook pasta for 5
minutes. Add carrots, cook for 1 minute. Add
broccoli, cook for 1 minute. Drain. Melt butter, stir fry
onion, garlic and corn for 3 minutes. Add chicken
stock, cream, salt, nutmeg and pepper. Cover and
bring to a boil. Add pasta mixture, cook for 1 minute
or until pasta is firm. Stir in cheese and chives and
basil.

LASAGNA PRIMAVERA

12 lasagna noodles, cooked

4 cups Alfredo sauce, prepared

3 cups frozen broccoli pieces, thawed

3 large carrots, coarsely shredded

1 -14 ounce can diced tomatoes, well drained

2 medium bell peppers, chopped

15 ounces ricotta cheese

½ cup Parmesan cheese, grated

1 egg

3 ½ cups mozzarella cheese, shredded

Mix broccoli, carrots, tomatoes and peppers in
bowl. Mix ricotta cheese, parmesan and egg
together in separate bowl.
Layer as follows in casserole dish:
4 noodles
1 cup Alfredo sauce
½ cheese and egg mixture
⅓ vegetable mixture
4 noodles
remaining cheese mixture
⅓ cup veggie mixture
Lasagna Primavera continued on next page......

1 cup Alfredo sauce
1 cup mozzarella cheese
remaining 4 noodles, vegetable mixture, Alfredo
sauce and top with mozzarella cheese.

Bake at 350° F. covered, for 30 minutes.
Remove the cover and bake for another 30
minutes. Let stand 10 minutes before serving.
(You can substitute vegetables such as spinach,
zucchini, red or yellow peppers or whatever you
have on hand.)

*You shouldn't go through life with a
catcher's mitt on both hands. You need to
throw something back.*

UNEXPECTED COMPANY LASAGNA

(This is a very easy version that can be put together in 20 minutes and served as a nice company dish.)

1 pound ground beef

1 medium onion

2 tins mushrooms (stems and pieces)

2 cans tomato soup

2- 8 ounce cans tomato paste

salt and pepper

3 teaspoons oregano

1 box precooked lasagna noodles

1½ cups of cottage cheese

2 cups of mozzarella cheese, grated

Brown ground beef in a frying pan, add chopped onion. When onion is beginning to brown add: paste, soup, mushrooms, salt, pepper and oregano. Let mixture simmer for a few minutes for flavours to blend. In a 9 x 13 inch pan, put ½ of meat mixture, top with a layer of noodles, the rest of the meat mixture, another layer of noodles, spread on the cottage cheese, another layer of noodles and top with a good thick layer of mozzarella cheese. Bake in 350° F. oven for 30 minutes. Serve with a loaf of garlic bread and a green salad and -Voila- not a bad supper at the last minute!

LENTIL STEW
(A super crock pot recipe.)

3 medium carrots, sliced

6 stalks celery, chopped

1 medium onion, chopped

½ teaspoon garlic salt

2 cups lentils

1 can tomatoes

2 cups vegetable juice

1 bay leaf

¼ teaspoon cayenne pepper

½ teaspoon oregano

½ teaspoon celery seed

½ teaspoon pepper

Mix all ingredients in a crock pot and simmer on low for at least 8 hours.

*For variation add browned, crumbled hamburger and 1 teaspoon chili powder instead of the cayenne pepper.

You know you are getting up there when your sweetie says "Let's go upstairs and make love and you answer, "Honey, I can't do both."

BARBEQUED SAUSAGES
(Delicious for dinner or brunch.)

1½ pounds pork breakfast sausages
Boil in enough water to cover for 10 minutes.
Rinse and drain.
Place sausages in small roaster or large
casserole.
1 small onion, chopped
2 stalks celery, diced
1 tin tomato soup
¼ cup white sugar
½ teaspoon dry mustard
½ teaspoon paprika
salt to taste

Mix together other ingredients and pour over
sausages. Bake at 350° F. for one hour.

BREADED VEAL OR PORK CUTLETS

6 veal or pork cutlets
2 tablespoons shortening
½ cup flour
1 teaspoon salt
¼ teaspoon pepper
2 eggs, slightly beaten
2 cups fine dry bread or cracker crumbs
2 tablespoons lemon juice

Mix together flour, salt and pepper. Dredge
cutlets in flour mixture, then dip in eggs, and coat
in breadcrumbs. In frying pan, heat shortening
until foamy. Add breaded cutlets and brown on
both sides. Reduce heat and cook for 10 minutes
or until meat is tender. Sprinkle with 2
tablespoons lemon juice. Serve immediately.
Serves 6.

FAVORITE CHOPS IN CASSEROLE

6 thick pork chops
salt and pepper to taste
4 apples, unpeeled
4 medium onions
½ cup brown sugar
2 teaspoons cinnamon
2 tablespoons butter
juice of 1 lemon
¼ cup water

Brown chops in heated skillet and add seasoning.
Arrange bed of chopped cored apples and sliced onions
in a deep casserole. Sprinkle with half the brown sugar
and cinnamon mixed. Place chops on these and sprinkle
with remaining sugar mix. Dot with butter.
Pour lemon juice and water over chops.
Cover and bake at 325°F. for 1 hour or more.
Uncover during last 10 minutes.

HOW MANY CAN YOU EAT RIBS?
(This is an absolute family favorite and no matter how many you make, the platter will be empty!)

3 pounds of back ribs
3 tablespoons canola oil
1 package dry onion soup mix
¼ cup vinegar
2 tablespoons brown sugar
1 cup ketchup
½ cup water
1 teaspoon prepared mustard
1 teaspoon salt

Preheat oven to 350° F. Cut ribs into serving size pieces and brown them in oil. Combine all other ingredients to make the sauce. Place browned ribs into a roaster and cover with sauce. Cover and bake in oven for 1½ to 2 hours. Check occasionally and rotate the ribs so they all get into the sauce. These can also be simmered on top of the stove in a heavy pot for the same length of time.
This should serve six but don't bother just making one batch!

Marriage is the triumph of imagination over intelligence. Just think, if it weren't for marriage, men would go through life thinking they had no faults at all.

FRUIT STUFFED PORK LOIN

¾ cup each pitted prunes and apricots, chopped
1 tablespoon gingerroot, grated
1 teaspoon orange rind, grated
1½ teaspoons ground cumin
½ teaspoon cinnamon
salt and pepper
4 pounds boneless pork loin roast
¼ cup packed brown sugar
2 teaspoons flour
2 teaspoons cider vinegar
1 teaspoon dry mustard
1 teaspoon cornstarch

In bowl, combine prunes, apricots, gingerroot, orange
rind , ½ teaspoon cumin, ½ teaspoon cinnamon and salt
and pepper to taste. Open up roast. Spoon stuffing
down center. Fold meat over and tie with kitchen string.
Place on rack in roasting pan. Combine sugar, flour,
vinegar, mustard and remaining cumin and spread over
roast. Bake in 325° F. oven for 1 ½ hours or until
Continued on next page..........

meat thermometer inserted into meat registers 160°F.
Transfer roast to platter, tent with foil.
Add ½ cup of water to roasting pan.
Cook over high heat, stirring to scrape up brown bits
from bottom of pan. Pour into saucepan; bring to boil
over medium-high heat. Mix cornstarch with 1
tablespoon water. Add to saucepan and cook stirring for
1 minute. Strain into gravy boat and serve with roast.
Makes 8 servings.

"Of course I don't look busy, I did it right the first time."

MAPLE RUM TENDERLOIN

2 pork tenderloins
1 teaspoon black pepper
1 teaspoon dried thyme
1 tablespoon margarine
2 oranges, unpeeled and thinly sliced
2 tablespoons cider vinegar
½ cup chicken stock
⅓ cup maple syrup
2 tablespoons dark rum
¼ teaspoon dried thyme

Season tenderloins well with pepper and 1 teaspoon
thyme. In frying pan, over medium-high heat, melt
margarine. Add tenderloins and brown well on all sides.
Line bottom of baking dish with orange slices. Place
pork on top of oranges and roast uncovered at 375° F.
for 40-60 minutes.

MAPLE-RUM SAUCE

Drain off any fat from frying pan; add vinegar and
bring to a boil scraping up any brown bits. Stir in stock,
maple syrup, rum and remaining thyme. Bring to boil,
reduce heat to low and simmer 10 minutes or until sauce
thickens. Slice pork tenderloin and serve on orange slices
with hot Maple Rum Sauce. Serves 6

Shown on previous page:

- Vinatarte...page 328
- Creamy Wheat Salad...page 115
- Saskatchewan Saskatoon Pie...page 282
- Rhubarb Meringue Torte...page 277

MARINATED PORK ROAST
(This roast may be done on the barbecue, on a spit or in a shallow roasting pan.)

4 pounds boneless pork loin roast
¼ cup honey
3 tablespoons brown sugar
¼ cup water
⅓ cup ketchup
2 tablespoons soya sauce
2 teaspoons paprika
1 teaspoon dry mustard
¼ teaspoon ginger

Combine all ingredients (except roast) in a saucepan. Bring to boil then cool. Marinate roast overnight in refrigerator. The next day, remove roast from marinade and place in a shallow roasting pan. Roast at 350°F. for 35 minutes on 1 side. Turn over and bake an additional 1 ½ hours. Baste with marinade while roasting.

PORK ROAST WITH ORANGE CHILI SAUCE
(A slow-cooker recipe)

4 slices bacon, finely chopped

3 pounds boneless pork roast, trimmed of excess fat

2 large onions, thinly sliced

3 cloves garlic, minced

2 jalapeño peppers, finely chopped

1½ tablespoons chili powder

1 teaspoon salt

1 teaspoon pepper

¼ cup all-purpose flour

1 tablespoon orange zest

1½ cups orange juice

2 bananas, thinly sliced

In a skillet, over medium — high heat, cook bacon until crisp. Remove with a slotted spoon to paper towel and drain thoroughly. In same pan, brown roast on all sides. Transfer to slow cooker. Remove all but 1 tablespoon fat from pan. Reduce heat to medium.

Continued on next page...........

194

PORK ROAST WITH ORANGE CHILI SAUCE

continued...............

Add onions and cook, stirring, until softened.
Add garlic, jalapeño peppers, chili powder, salt and
pepper and cook, stirring, for 1 minute.
Sprinkle flour over mixture and cook, stirring, for 1
minute. Add orange zest, orange juice and bananas and
cook, stirring to scrape up any brown bits and mashing
bananas into sauce. Stir in bacon pieces.
Pour mixture over pork. Cover and cook on low for 8
—10 hours or on high for 4 —5 hours, until meat is
very tender. Serve with rice.

It is good to be a woman:
No fashion faux pas we make, could ever rival
the Speedo.
We can congratulate our teammate without
ever touching her rear end.
If we marry someone 20 years younger, we are
aware that we will look like an idiot.
We can scare male bosses with the mysterious
gynecological disorder excuses.

SAVOURY PORK CHOPS
WITH SAUERKRAUT

(A delicious slow-cooker recipe.)

1 tablespoon canola oil

6 thick-cut pork chops

1 tablespoon flour

1 teaspoon salt

½ teaspoon pepper

pinch cayenne pepper

1 teaspoon dry mustard

2 cups sauerkraut (if using store bought sauerkraut rinse thoroughly under cold water before adding to recipe to reduce the vinegary taste)

1 Granny Smith apple, peeled, cored and grated

½ cup condensed chicken broth (undiluted)

In a skillet, heat oil over medium-high heat.

Add pork chops, in batches, and brown on both sides.

Transfer to slow cooker.

Sprinkle with flour, salt, pepper, cayenne and dry mustard.

In a bowl, combine sauerkraut and grated apple.

Spread over top of pork. Add chicken stock.

Cover and cook on low for 5 hours or on high for 2 ½ hours.

SWEET AND SOUR RIBS

2 pounds side or back pork ribs
1½ cups brown sugar
2 tablespoons cornstarch
½ teaspoon salt
½ cup vinegar
1½ cups water
Coat ribs with flour and fry till browned. In saucepan bring to a boil: sugar, cornstarch, salt, vinegar and water. Preheat oven to 350° F. Place ribs in roaster and pour sauce over, bake for 1 hour. Serve with rice.

I am out of estrogen and I have a gun!

BAKED SALMON

(Everyone will rave about this salmon
and it is so easy to prepare.)

½ large salmon fillet (about 3 pounds)
1 cup brown sugar
½ cup lemon juice

Cover a cookie sheet with foil, spray with non-stick oil. Place salmon fillet on foil. Spread sugar all over top of salmon. Drizzle with lemon juice. Bring foil together, wrap and seal. Bake at 350° F. for 1½ hours.

"Old age ain't no place for sissies."
Bette Davis

STUFFED BAKED SALMON
(Nice served with our Breast Rice Pilaf.)

1 thick filet of salmon (sliced in half)
  or 2 thinner filets
¼ cup cream cheese, softened
2½ cups mushrooms, sliced
1 tablespoon canola oil
1 tablespoon balsamic vinegar
1 -6 ounce package spinach, cooked, drained and chopped
¼ teaspoon lemon pepper
1 lemon sliced (or drizzle of lemon juice)

Sauté mushrooms in oil until lightly browned. Place in bowl and sprinkle with balsamic vinegar. Mix in the chopped spinach. Spread cream cheese over fillets. Top with the spinach mixture; place other fillet on top and tie together with string. Sprinkle on lemon pepper and lemon juice or lay the lemon slices on top. Place in covered roasting pan. Bake at 400° F. for 40 minutes. Slice to serve.

FETTUCCINI SEAFOOD SAUCE

1 green pepper
1 red pepper
1 cup green onions
2 cups fresh mushrooms, sliced
2 tomatoes, chopped
1 teaspoon dill weed
1 cup heavy cream
2 -8 ounce packages cream cheese
2 cans crab meat
1 cup frozen baby shrimp

Chop peppers, onions and sauté lightly. Add the mushrooms and sauté just for another minute — don't let mushrooms or peppers soften too much. Remove from pan and cook shrimp (deveined and tail removed) until pink or if precooked, heat through. In a big pot melt cheese and add cream and dill weed. Add peppers, onions and mushrooms, shrimp and crab. Heat mixture — add chopped tomatoes just a minute before serving. Serve over cooked fettuccini with garlic bread or bread sticks. A side dish of more chopped tomatoes and green onions is nice in case people want to add more.

SHRIMP AND PASTA

(Sautéed shrimp with fettuccine in an Alfredo-
type sauce. Fresh Parmesan cheese
makes this really special.)

⅓ cup clarified butter
14 large shrimp, peeled and deveined
2 teaspoons fresh or dried parsley
1 teaspoon black pepper
¼ cup dry white wine
5 ounces fettuccine, cooked to box directions
½ cup half and half cream
1 cup Parmesan cheese, freshly grated

Heat butter in a medium or large sauté pan, add
shrimp, parsley and pepper, and cook until
shrimp are done, but don't overcook. Remove
from the pan, then deglaze the pan with white
wine over low heat. Add fettuccine and shrimp
and stir. Add cream, stir again and then toss
with Parmesan cheese. Place into microwave
until it steams and serve immediately. Serves 4.
*In small portions can be served as an appetizer.

SHRIMP VEGETABLE CREOLE
(This dish will take you back to the Carribean!)

1 cup onion, chopped
1 cup celery, chopped
½ each: green, red, yellow peppers, chopped
2 garlic cloves, minced
6 tablespoons margarine
2 -16 ounce canned tomatoes
2 -8 ounce cans tomato sauce
1 tablespoon salt
2 teaspoons sugar
2 teaspoons chili powder
2 tablespoons Worcestershire sauce
Dash of tabasco
4 teaspoons cornstarch
cooked shrimp, about 40

Sauté in margarine until tender, not brown;
onion, peppers, celery and garlic. Add
tomatoes, tomato sauce, salt, sugar, chili powder,
Worcestershire sauce and tabasco. Simmer,
uncovered for 45 minutes. Mix cornstarch in 1
tablespoon cold water and add to sauce. Cook
and stir until mixture thickens and bubbles. Add
shrimp. Serve over white rice.

ALL AFTERNOON STEAK SUPPER

(This is a great recipe because you can throw it in the oven at noon and supper is ready when you walk in the door after work)

2 pounds of round or sirloin steak
1 package dry onion soup mix
1 can cream of mushroom soup
½ can water

Cut the steak into serving size pieces and place in a small roaster or casserole dish. Sprinkle the package of onion soup mix over the meat and add the can of cream of mushroom soup diluted with water. Cover and bake at 300° F. for five hours or 350° F. for four hours. Gravy is nice and brown- great with potatoes or noodles.

"My sister's and brother's faults I will lay on the shore of the sea, forever, to be erased, and their virtues I will inscribe on the tablets of my heart."
From the Elk's 11th hour service

FAVOURITE BEEF STROGANOFF

1 large onion, sliced
2 tablespoons canola oil
2 pounds sirloin or round steak cut into cubes
½ cup flour
1 teaspoon salt
½ teaspoon pepper
1 teaspoon dry mustard
1 cup beef bouillon
extra water, if needed
2 tablespoons tomato paste
3 tablespoons dry wine
1 can or 1 cup fresh mushrooms
2 cups sour cream
rice or noodles for serving

Combine flour, salt, pepper and dry mustard.
Brown the onion in the oil, and add meat which has
been dipped in flour mixture. Brown well. Add bouillon
and extra water, if needed. Simmer about 1 hour. Stir
in tomato paste and wine. Add mushrooms and simmer
a few minutes. Stir in sour cream just before serving and
serve over rice.

GREY CUP SWISS STEAK

(An easy crowd pleaser that you can put on to cook and enjoy the game!)

2 ½ to 3 pounds of sirloin or round steak
1 teaspoon salt
¼ teaspoon pepper
¼ cup flour
2 tablespoons canola oil
1 cup undrained tomatoes, cut into pieces
1 cup tomato sauce
1 envelope dry brown gravy mix
1 large onion, sliced

Cut meat into serving sized pieces. Combine salt, pepper and flour in a shallow bowl or plastic bag and coat the meat in seasoned flour. Brown meat in oil in a large frying pan over medium-high heat. Drain excess fat. Add remaining ingredients. (Transfer to Dutch oven at this point- frying pan is just too full.) Simmer covered 1 ½ to 2 hours until meat is tender.
Great served over noodles.
For company you can make this ahead as directed, simmering until tender and then refrigerate. When ready to serve, heat thoroughly.

ORANGE GINGER STIR FRY

1½ pounds sirloin steak, sliced into thin strips

3 tablespoons soy sauce

1 cup milk

1 beef bouillon cube or 1 teaspoon instant bouillon

½ cup orange juice and 2 teaspoons orange zest, grated

2 tablespoons canola oil

1 tablespoon butter or margarine

2 cups mushrooms, sliced

1 cup carrots, grated

1 red pepper, cut in strips

2 cups broccoli florets

4 green onions

1 tablespoon ginger

2 cloves garlic or 2 teaspoons garlic, minced

2 tablespoons cornstarch dissolved in 2 tablespoons water

Put steak strips in half of the soy sauce and set aside. In a medium bowl, combine milk and bouillon, add orange juice, zest, and remaining soy sauce, set aside. In a large frying pan or wok, heat the oil over medium high heat. Add beef strips and fry until beef is no longer pink, remove from heat and set aside. Add butter to frying pan and sauté the mushrooms. Add vegetables, ginger and garlic. Stir for 3 minutes. Add milk mixture and beef and stir. Bring to a boil. Add cornstarch and water and mix into stir-fry sauce until sauce thickens. Serve over Chinese noodles or rice.

ROUND-UP STEAK

2 pounds round steak, 1-inch thick

¼ cup flour

½ teaspoon salt

⅛ teaspoon pepper

¼ cup margarine or bacon drippings

1 -19 ounce can tomatoes

1 teaspoon sugar

1 teaspoon dry mustard

1 teaspoon Worcestershire sauce

1 cup onions, chopped

1 clove garlic, minced

Mix together flour, salt and pepper. Pound the flour mixture into meat, using meat hammer or edge of saucer. Cut into 8 serving pieces. In large skillet brown the steak in hot drippings. Add onion and garlic. Stir in tomatoes, sugar, dry mustard and Worcestershire sauce. Cover and simmer over low heat for about one hour or until meat is tender. Remove meat to platter. Thicken gravy with mixture of flour water. Pour over meat. Serves 8.

SAUCY SWISS STEAK
(Such a good slow cooker
recipe, you'll want seconds.)

1 tablespoon canola oil
2 pounds round steak cut in serving pieces
2 medium onions, finely chopped
1 carrot, thinly sliced
1 stalk celery, thinly sliced
½ teaspoon salt
¼ teaspoon pepper
2 tablespoons flour
1 —28 ounce can plum tomatoes, drained and chopped
½ cup juice reserved
1 tablespoon Worcestershire sauce
1 bay leaf

In a skillet, heat oil. Add steak and brown on both
sides. Transfer to slow cooker. Reduce heat to medium
— low. Add onion, carrots, celery, salt and pepper to
pan. Cover and cook until vegetables are softened about
8 minutes. Sprinkle flour over vegetables and cook for 1
minute, stirring. Add tomatoes, reserved juice and
Worcestershire sauce. Bring to a boil, stirring until
thickened. Add bay leaf. Pour tomato mixture over
steak and cook on Low for 8 to 10 hours or on High 4
— 5 hours, until meat is tender. Discard bay leaf.

STEAK BAKE
(Serve these with the Tangy Cheese Muffins in this book! They are the perfect complement!)

1½ pounds sirloin steak

⅓ cup flour

1 teaspoon salt

¼ teaspoon pepper

3 tablespoons molasses

3 tablespoons soy sauce

1 small onion, sliced

1 green pepper slivered

1 -19 ounce can tomatoes

1 -10 ounce can mushrooms pieces and stems

1 -19 ounce can green beans,drained

Cut meat into narrow strips and place in 2 ½ quart casserole. Sprinkle with flour, salt and pepper.
Toss to coat meat, leaving excess flour in bottom of casserole. Bake uncovered 400° F. for 20 minutes.
Remove from oven and mix in onion, drained mushrooms, vegetables, molasses and soy sauce. Cover and return to 400°F. oven and bake another 30 minutes.

OVEN BEEF STEW
(Great served in hollowed-out dinner buns!)

1 ½ pounds stewing beef
½ cup flour
½ teaspoon paprika
1 teaspoon salt
½ teaspoon pepper
¼ cup butter or margarine
⅛ teaspoon garlic salt
2 chicken or beef bouillon cubes
2 ½ cups boiling water
1 large onion
6 carrots

Place beef in bag with flour, salt, paprika, pepper.
Pour all into frying pan with melted margarine.
Sear on all sides. Add garlic salt. Put in casserole.
Dissolve bouillon cubes in frying pan with water.
Pour over meat. Add raw carrots cut in 1 inch pieces
and onion cut in eighths.
Cover and bake 250°F. for 3 – 3 ½ hours.

QUICK AND EASY
DELICIOUS STEW

2 pounds stewing meat
1 tablespoon cornstarch
1 package onion soup mix
¼ cup brown sugar
1 can beef consommé soup
1 can mushroom soup
1 ½ cups carrots, cut in chunks
3 stalks of sliced celery, sliced
1 cup peas
5 medium potatoes, peeled and cut in chunks

Combine meat, soups, cornstarch and brown
sugar in a roaster. Add carrots, celery, peas
and potatoes. Cover roaster. Bake at 250° F.
for 4 hours. Uncover and bake at 350° F. for
approximately 15 minutes.

*"The best portion of a good person's life is
the little, daily, unremembered acts of
kindness and love"*
Marcus Cicero

Minimizing Your Risk

There are risk factors for breast cancer that you have no control over, such as your age, your family history or your reproductive history. But you can substantially reduce your risk by making positive changes to your lifestyle.

- Be physically active. Studies show that even moderate physical activity can reduce your risk by 30 to 40 per cent. Choose an exercise or an activity that makes you feel warm and breathe harder (such as brisk walking) for 30 to 60 minutes, at least four times a week.
- Lose excess weight. A 5-kg (about 11 pounds) increase in body weight can be a significant breast cancer risk factor, especially after menopause.
- Eat more fruits and vegetables. A lower-fat diet that includes five to ten servings of fruits and vegetables every day will minimize your risk for several types of cancer, including breast cancer.
- Limit your intake of alcohol. Women who drink alcohol have a slightly higher risk. The more you drink, the greater your risk.

Health Canada, November 2002, Reproduced with the permission of the Minister of Public Works and Government Services Canada, 2004.

Vegetables and Side Dishes

"'There will never be a generation of great men until there has been a generation of free women — of free mothers." Robert G. Ingersoll

BAKED BEANS
(Great side dish to serve at a barbecue.)

1 -14-ounce can seasoned green beans
1 -14-ounce can kidney beans
1 -14-ounce can lima beans
1 -14-ounce can of pork and beans
1 can of mushrooms, stems and pieces
1 pound bacon, diced
1 large onion, chopped
1 cup brown sugar
1 bottle of chili sauce

Mix the beans together. Fry bacon and onion. Drain off fat and add to bean mixture. Stir in the brown sugar and chili sauce. Pour into a large casserole and bake at 350°F. for 1 ½ hours.

"The measure of a person's real character is what he would do if he knew he would never be found out" Thomas Macauley

THE "BREAST" RICE PILAFF

(We multiplied this recipe by 10 for each roaster and did five roasters for our breast cancer banquet. It was a nice complement to the chicken and was very easy to do.)

½ cup onion, chopped
2 stalks celery, chopped
¼ cup red pepper
2 tablespoons oil
2 cups hot water
1 can mushrooms, sliced
1 cup short grain rice
2 tablespoons chicken bouillon

Sauté onion, celery, red pepper in the oil over medium heat until onion is transparent.

Mix with remaining ingredients in casserole dish and bake at 350° F. for 1 hour.

Do you know what would have happened if it had been Three Wise Women instead of Three Wise Men? They would have asked directions, arrived on time, helped deliver the baby, cleaned the stable, made a casserole and brought practical gifts.

BROCCOLI CASSEROLE

1 cup rice cooked in 2 ½ cups of water
2 bunches broccoli, cooked and drained

Sauté:
½ cup margarine
½ cup celery, sliced
½ cup onions, chopped

1 -10 ounce can of mushroom soup
1 cup Cheese Whiz

Add chopped broccoli to cooked rice. To sautéed
mixture add the mushroom soup and cheese whiz and
blend. Mix the sautéed mixture to the rice and broccoli.
Put in casserole and bake at 350° F. for 30
minutes.
Note: If you like a crunchy topping, crush soda
crackers and sprinkle on top before baking.

When women are depressed they either eat or go
shopping. Men invade another country.
                      Elayne Boosler

BRUSSEL SPROUTS
WITH PEAR AND MUSTARD SAUCE

4 cups brussel sprouts
1 ripe pear, peeled and sliced
½ cup unsalted butter
2 teaspoons Dijon mustard
salt and freshly ground pepper

Trim the brussel sprouts of outside leaves and stems. Cut an X in the stem end. Rinse in cold water, then cook in boiling salted water for 10 minutes or until just tender. While the brussel sprouts are cooking, gently sauté the pear slices in 4 tablespoons of butter until heated through. Stir in the mustard and add the remaining 4 tablespoons of butter. When the brussel sprouts are cooked, toss them with the pear and mustard sauce. Season to taste with salt and pepper.
Serves 6.

"If you think fisherman are the biggest liars in the world, ask a jogger how far he runs every morning."   *Larry Johnson*

BUFFET POTATO CASSEROLE

6 russet potatoes, peeled and diced
½ cup butter
1 ½ cups swiss cheese, shredded
2 tablespoons green onions, finely chopped
salt and pepper to taste
1 ¼ cups milk
¾ cup fine dry bread crumbs
⅓ cup parmesan cheese, grated
2 tablespoons parsley, chopped
3 tablespoons butter, melted

Cook potatoes in a small amount of boiling salted water.
Drain and break up into small pieces with a fork. Add
½ cup butter, swiss cheese, onion, salt and pepper.
Toss with a fork to combine. Spread mixture in a 2
quart shallow rectangular baking dish. Pour milk over
potato mixture. Combine bread crumbs, parmesan
cheese, parsley and 3 tablespoons melted butter.
Sprinkle over potatoes. Bake in preheated 375° F.
oven 20 – 25 minutes or until hot and topping has
browned.

TURNIP CARROT CASSEROLE

1 medium turnip, peeled and cut up
8-10 medium carrots, peeled and cut up
1 teaspoon salt

¼ cup melted butter
2 cups Velveeta cheese, cubed
salt and pepper to taste

2 tablespoons butter
1 cup breadcrumbs

Cook and mash together turnip and carrots. Add salt and pepper to taste. Mix in melted butter and Velveeta cheese. Put in a buttered 6-quart casserole. Melt butter and add breadcrumbs. Sprinkle on top of mixture and bake at 350° F. for ½ hour.

"Clever is when you believe only half of what you hear. Brilliant is when you know which half to believe."   *Orben*

CHEESY CARROT BAKE

2 pounds carrots

2 tablespoons butter

1 medium onion, chopped

salt + pepper to taste

2 cups cheddar cheese, shredded

parsley

buttered bread crumbs

Peel, slice and cook carrots in boiling water until tender. Drain and mash well. Add butter, onion and cheese and seasonings. Turn into a casserole dish. Sprinkle top with buttered crumbs before baking. Bake at 350° F. for 40 minutes, until bubbling. Garnish with parsley. Serves 8.

CHEESE AND ASPARAGUS PUFF

4 large or 5 medium eggs

2 cups milk

½ teaspoon salt

pinch of pepper

1 cup fine cracker crumbs

10 ounces Edam or Gouda cheese cut into ¼ inch cubes

1 pound fresh or canned asparagus, or frozen ½ inch pieces

2 tablespoons butter, melted

Into large casserole break eggs and beat with whisk. Add all remaining ingredients except asparagus and butter. Stir until thoroughly blended. Arrange asparagus on top- drizzle with melted butter. Bake at 350°F. for 50-60 minutes. Serves 6.

219

CARROT CASSEROLE

2 cups sliced carrots (cooked slightly)

½ medium onion, chopped

2 tablespoons margarine

1 –10 ounce can, cream of mushroom soup

½ cup Cheese Whiz

1 package Chicken stovetop stuffing, prepared

Sauté onions in margarine. Add soup and Cheese Whiz. Add to slightly cooked carrots. Put in an 8 x 8 inch pan. Top with prepared stuffing and bake at 325° F. for approximately 30 minutes.

CORN MEAL CASSEROLE

1 can cream corn

2 eggs, beaten

½ teaspoon salt

1 cup cheddar cheese, grated

⅛ cup butter, melted

½ cup cornmeal

1 cup sour cream

¼ cup green onions, or regular onion, chopped

dill to taste

Combine all ingredients. Pour into a casserole dish which has been sprayed with non-stick spray. Bake at 350° F. for 1 hour.

CAULIFLOWER AU GRATIN

6 cups cauliflower, cut into florets

⅓ cup red pepper, coarsely chopped

2 tablespoons butter

3 tablespoons all-purpose flour

1 teaspoon garlic, minced

1¼ cups milk or half and half

½ cups cheddar cheese, grated

¼ cup Parmesan cheese

2 tablespoons dill or parsley

¼ teaspoon pepper and ½ teaspoon salt

Topping:

3 tablespoons dried bread crumbs

2 tablespoons Parmesan cheese

Preheat oven to 375° F. Grease 1½ quart casserole
dish. In pot of boiling water, cook cauliflower until tender
3 to 5 minutes. Place in casserole dish and sprinkle with
red pepper. In frying pan melt butter, add flour and
garlic; cook stirring over low heat for one minute. Pour
in milk and simmer for 2 to 3 minutes until thickened.
Add cheeses, dill, salt and pepper and cook stirring
until cheese is melted. Pour over cauliflower. Mix bread
crumbs with Parmesan cheese and sprinkle over the top.
Bake uncovered for 25 to 30 minutes.

CURRIED CORN

2 cups corn (frozen or fresh)
2 tablespoons butter
3 tablespoons onion, finely chopped
½ teaspoon curry powder
½ cup sour cream
½ teaspoon salt
⅛ teaspoon pepper

Melt butter, add corn, onion and curry powder. Sauté.
Cover and simmer slowly about 10 minutes until tender,
stirring often.
Add sour cream, salt and pepper.
Heat until warm and serve.

*"There's no point in burying a hatchet if you're going
to put up a marker on the site."*
Sydney Harris

DELUXE PEAS

1 tablespoon butter or margarine
1 teaspoon chicken bouillon powder
2 tablespoons water
1 ½ cups mushrooms, sliced
1 cup celery, sliced diagonally
½ teaspoon dried dill weed
¼ teaspoon curry powder
2 cups peas
¾ cup water chestnuts, sliced
2 tablespoons red bell pepper, chopped

In a large skillet over medium heat; melt butter, stir in chicken bouillon powder, water, mushrooms, celery and seasonings; cook for about 6 minutes or until vegetables are almost tender. Stir in peas; cook, uncovered, for 2 minutes. Add water chestnuts and pepper, cook, stirring occasionally, for about 1 minute or until heated through. Serves 6.

"One man can be a crucial ingredient on a team but one man cannot make a team."
Kareen Abdul Jabbar

DUMPLINGS FOR MEAT STEW

2 cups flour

3 teaspoons baking powder

½ teaspoon salt

2 tablespoons canola oil

1 cup milk

3 tablespoons finely chopped fresh parsley (or ⅓ as much dried) may be added to dry ingredients.

Mix ingredients, only until combined.

Drop into a slowly boiling stew with a tablespoon.

Cover container tightly.

Cook on low/medium heat for 12 – 15 minutes.

Serve at once.

"We did not change as we grew older, we just became more clearly ourselves." Lynn Hall

GOURMET WILD RICE CASSEROLE

8 ounces wild rice
1 cup boiling water
1 cup medium cheddar cheese, grated
1 cup canned tomatoes, diced
1 cup mushrooms, fried
½ cup margarine
1 teaspoon garlic, fresh or grated
1 teaspoon seasoning salt
½ cup celery, chopped

Place rice in double boiler, cover with boiling water and cook for one hour or until rice is tender. Add remaining ingredients. Place in two quart buttered casserole and bake for one hour at 350° F. This rice dish can be prepared the day before and baked just before serving.

The noblest vengeance is to forgive - English Proverb

GREEN BEAN ALMONDINE
(Sweet and Sour Green Beans)

3 slices bacon
½ cup brown sugar
½ cup vinegar
1 small onion, thinly sliced
½ teaspoon dry mustard
½ teaspoon salt
32 ounces frozen French-style green beans
(cooked and drained) or canned beans, drained
½ cup slivered almonds

Fry the bacon until crisp and set aside. Into the
skillet of bacon drippings add the sugar, vinegar,
dry mustard and salt. Separate the onion into
rings and place in the skillet. Add the drained
beans and almonds. Cover and simmer for
about 25 minutes. Sprinkle the crumbled bacon
over the beans when ready to serve.
Serves 6 to 8.

*"Make sure you have finished speaking before the
audience has finished listening"* Dorothy Sarnoff

LAZY PEROGIE CASSEROLE

15 lasagna noodles

2 cups cottage cheese

2 eggs

¼ teaspoon onion salt

1 cup cheddar cheese, grated

2 cups warm mashed potatoes

¼ teaspoon salt

1 ¼ cups onion, finely chopped

⅛ teaspoon pepper

1 cup margarine

Cook noodles as directed on box. Drain and pat dry with paper towel. Line bottom of 9 x 13 inch pan with 5 noodles. Mix cottage cheese, eggs, and onion salt together. Spread over noodles. Cover with another layer of noodles. Mix cheddar cheese, potatoes, salt, ¼ cup chopped onion, and pepper. Spread over noodles. Cover with layer of remaining noodles. Melt butter or margarine in frying pan and sauté 1 cup of onions until clear and soft. Pour over noodles. Cover and bake for 30 minutes at 350° F. Remove from oven and let stand for 10 –15 minutes before serving. Serve with sour cream.

LEMON POTATOES

6 cups potatoes, peeled and quartered

2 cups water

¼ cup chicken in a mug

3 tablespoons flour

½ cup lemon juice

½ teaspoon garlic powder

¼ cup melted butter

Put potatoes in casserole. Mix ingredients and pour over. Place in 325° F. oven until well cooked, about 1 ½ hours. *Add water if sauce is too thick.

ORIENTAL GREEN BEANS

2 (1 kg.) pound package green beans

4 tablespoons soya sauce

1 -10 ounce can sliced mushrooms or 1 pound of fresh mushrooms

⅓ cup slivered almonds

Combine ingredients and place in a 2 quart casserole dish. Bake for 30 to 40 minutes at 350° F. Remove from oven and add 2 tablespoons of mayonnaise.

Mix and serve.

Shown on previous page:

- Pinwheel Bread... page 61
- Harvest Bread... page 56
- Maple Grove Buns... page 68
- Clam Chowder... page 97
- Wholesome Lentil Soup... page 109

OVEN ROASTED ROSEMARY POTATOES

3 large sweet potatoes
3 large white potatoes
½ cup water
2 tablespoons canola oil
2 teaspoons dried rosemary

Peel potatoes and cut into ⅛ inch thick slices.
Spread 1 tablespoon of oil over the bottom of a 9 x 13
inch baking pan. Pack sweet and white potatoes tightly
in alternating rows. Add water. Drizzle, with the other
tablespoon of oil. Sprinkle with rosemary. Bake at
350°F. for 30 to 45 minutes or until tender.

**"If you want breakfast in bed, sleep
in the kitchen."**

NACHINKA

(A cornmeal spoon bread that complements many entrees, especially poultry.)

2 cups whole milk
½ cup butter
1 tablespoon onion, minced
1 tablespoon sugar
1 teaspoon salt
⅛ teaspoon pepper
¾ cup yellow cornmeal
3 eggs plus ½ cup milk
⅛ cup canola oil

Scald 2 cups milk. Sauté onion in butter. Add onions and butter, sugar, salt and pepper to milk. Over medium heat; slowly add the cornmeal to milk mixture stirring to prevent lumps. Stir until mixture thickens. Cool. Beat 3 eggs with ½ cup milk and add to cornmeal mixture. Stir in oil. Mix well. Pour into a one quart greased casserole. Bake uncovered in a 350° F. oven for about 60 minutes. Serve immediately.

POTATO CASSEROLE

8 large yellow flesh potatoes, cooked and mashed
1 package cream cheese, softened
1 cup sour cream
¼ cup butter
1 teaspoon salt
¼ teaspoon pepper
paprika
parsley, chopped

In a large bowl, combine mashed potatoes, cream
cheese, sour cream, butter, salt and pepper.
Beat together until smooth and fluffy.
Spread evenly in a greased 2 quart casserole.
Sprinkle with paprika and chopped parsley.
Bake in 350°F. for 20 minutes or until heated
through. Serves 8.

Habits are the first cobwebs, then cables.
Spanish Proverb

PEROGY DOUGH AND FILLING

(This is a good recipe for beginners or to hand down to the next generation. These are lots of work but soooo worth it!)

5 cups flour

1 tablespoon salt

½ cup canola oil

2 cups lukewarm water

Mix and knead ingredients together into soft, smooth dough. Put in a bowl, cover and let rest for 1 hour. Roll out small amounts of dough quite thinly on a floured surface. Cut into 2 – 2 ½ -inch squares or circles. Place about 1 teaspoon of filling onto the middle of each square. Fold over, forming triangles, pinch the edges together well to seal the filling. Place on cookie sheet with clean tea towel. *May be frozen at this point. See instructions below.

Perogy Filling:

5-6 cups potatoes, mashed

½ cup margarine

1 medium onion, chopped

1 teaspoon pepper

1 teaspoon salt

continued on the next page......................

PEROGY DOUGH AND FILLING continued...

1 cup cottage cheese or grated cheddar cheese or
¼ cup cheese whiz (more if desired)

Sauté onion in margarine; add to mashed
potatoes. Add salt, pepper and cheese of your
choice. Mash really well. Cool mixture
thoroughly before making perogies. To cook
perogies, drop into a pot with 12 cups salted,
boiling water. Only cook 2 ½ - 3 dozen at one
time. Stir with wooden spoon a few times to
prevent sticking to the bottom. Boil steadily for 4
to 5 minutes. Drain in colander. Place in a
deep dish, sprinkle generously with melted butter
or fried onions in butter. Toss gently to coat the
perogies to keep them from sticking together.
Serve with sour cream, sautéed onions in butter
or mushroom sauce. *To freeze the perogies,
place them on a cookie sheet lined with plastic (2
layers to a sheet). The perogies don't stick to the
plastic when frozen and are easier to pack in
plastic bags. Makes about 10 dozen.

MUSHROOM SAUCE FOR PEROGIES

4 tablespoons butter
2 tablespoons onion, finely chopped
3 tablespoons flour
¼ teaspoon salt
⅛ teaspoon pepper
1-10 ounce can mushroom soup
1 cup milk or half and half cream
1 can mushrooms with juice
Dried dill weed, optional

Melt butter in a pan. Add chopped onion and cook slowly until transparent, 2 to 3 minutes. Add flour (working well into the margarine and onions) salt, pepper, mushroom soup and milk. Cook, stirring constantly over low heat until thickened. Add mushrooms with juice. This recipe can be stretched for a large crowd by adding another can of mushroom soup and more milk. If too thin, thicken with a little cornstarch.

"It's easier to leave angry words unspoken, then to mend a heart whose words have broken."
Unknown

POTATO PANCAKES
(Great served for breakfast or lunch.)

½ cup flour
1 teaspoon salt
1 teaspoon baking powder
⅛ teaspoon pepper
1 tablespoon onion, grated
1 egg
½ cup milk
2 tablespoons butter, melted
2 cups raw potatoes, grated
dash of garlic powder

Mix dry ingredients.
Add eggs, milk, melted butter, grated potatoes and onions. Stir. Drop by spoonfuls and flatten on non-stick pan. Fry until brown on each side. Serve with cottage cheese, sour cream or a sweet fruit sauce like chokecherry syrup.

"You don't stop laughing because you grow old, your grow old because you stop laughing." Michael Pritchard

235

SCALLOPED TOMATOES

6 peeled medium tomatoes

½ cup chopped onion

½ cup chopped celery

2 tablespoons butter or margarine

¾ teaspoon salt

¼ teaspoon pepper

¼ teaspoon oregano

½ cup buttered cracker crumbs

Cut tomatoes in quarters. Sauté onion and celery in butter. Combine with tomatoes and seasonings.
Turn half the mixture into a greased baking dish. Sprinkle with half the crumbs. Add remaining tomato mixture and top with remaining crumbs. Bake uncovered at 375°F. until lightly browned (about 25 minutes).

SIMPLE ZUCCHINI CASSEROLE

4 cups zucchini cut into chunks

1 can tomato soup

½ teaspoon oregano

1 cup mozzarella cheese, grated

Peel and chunk zucchini. Place the above in a casserole dish and bake for 30 minutes at 350° F.   Before serving top with grated mozzarella cheese. Place back in oven for 5 minutes to melt cheese. Serves 6.

SPINACH AND WILD RICE CASSEROLE

1 cup wild rice, cooked
1 cup cheddar cheese, shredded
2 tablespoon onion, minced
3 eggs, beaten
½ cup milk
2 tablespoons butter, melted
1 teaspoon Worcestershire sauce
⅛ teaspoon thyme
½ teaspoon garlic salt
pepper to taste
¾ pound of chopped spinach, drained
½ cup shredded cheddar cheese for topping

Mix rice, 1 cup cheese and onion. Mix remaining ingredients, except ½ cup shredded cheese. Add to first mixture. Put into greased casserole dish. Top with remaining ½ cup cheese. Bake at 350° F. for 30 minutes. Let sit for 5 minutes before serving.

"Love doesn't just sit there, like a stone. It has to be made, like bread; remade all the time, made new" Ursula K LeGuin

STUFFED BAKED POTATOES

6 baking potatoes
½ cup butter
½ cup half and half cream
2 packages chicken soup base
½ teaspoon dill weed
1 teaspoon parsley
1 tablespoon minced onion
cheddar cheese, grated
Salt and pepper

*You can adjust the above ingredients to taste.
Bake the potatoes. (Cook extra to fill the shells
well.) When they are done, split them lengthwise
and scoop the potatoes out of the shells. While
they are still hot, whip the potatoes with the
butter, cream, and soup base, salt and pepper.
Add onion, dill weed and parsley. Add more
cream if necessary. Spoon the mixture back into
the shells. Sprinkle the tops with grated cheddar
cheese and bake until cheese is melted and
bubbly. Serves 6.

WHOLESOME TASTY BEAN BAKE
(A great slow-cooker recipe.)

8 bacon strips, diced

2 medium onions, thinly sliced

1 cup brown sugar

½ cup vinegar

1 teaspoon salt

1 teaspoon mustard powder

½ teaspoon garlic powder

1 can kidney beans

1 can pinto beans

1 can lima beans

1 can chick peas

1 can baked beans in tomato sauce (undrained)

Rinse and drain: kidney, pinto, lima beans and chick peas. Cook bacon until crisp, drain. In drippings sauté onions until tender. Add brown sugar, vinegar, salt, mustard and garlic powder. In slow cooker, combine beans and onion mixture. Cover and cook on high for about 3 hours.

"Life is under no obligation to give us what we expect"
Margaret Mitchell

YOWSA SALSA

18 large tomatoes, skinned and diced

8 medium onions, chopped

3 peppers, yellow, green and red, chopped

2 ¾ cups vinegar

8 Macintosh apples, peeled and grated

8 cloves garlic, chopped fine

4 ounces of jalepeno peppers, chopped

1 10-ounce can kernel corn

1 10-ounce can black beans, rinsed

6 tablespoons coarse salt

¾ tablespoons dried mustard

1 ½ teaspoons cayenne pepper

1 -12 ounce can tomato paste

⅔ cup sugar

½ teaspoon paprika

Mix first 7 ingredients in large stockpot. Simmer
for 1 hour or until slightly thickened. Add the
beans and corn. Stir in salt, mustard, pepper,
tomato paste and sugar. Boil for 3 minutes.
Place in hot jars and seal. This will yield 14
pints. Let stand for 24 hours. Then enjoy.
(Note: Don't want to peel tomatoes? Use a
large commercial can of diced tomatoes or 5
28-ounce cans of diced tomatoes.)

MIXED VEGETABLE RICE BAKE

(A great side dish or it can be served as a veggie meal.)

1 cup water mixed with 1 cup of milk
1 cup long grain rice
1 tablespoon butter
1 medium onion, chopped
2 teaspoons garlic, minced
4 cups of frozen mixed vegetables
3 eggs beaten with ½ cup milk
1 ½ cups cheddar cheese, grated
¾ teaspoon salt
dash Tabasco sauce
¼ cup dried bread crumbs
¼ cup Parmesan cheese

In saucepan bring water and milk to a boil, add rice, cover and reduce to simmer for 20 minutes. In frying pan sauté onion and garlic in butter until tender. Increase heat to high and add frozen vegetables. Cook for about 5 minutes until thawed. Mix eggs with ½ cup milk and stir into rice. Add cheese, salt and Tabasco. Combine with vegetables and transfer to a 2 quart casserole dish. Sprinkle with breadcrumbs and Parmesan cheese. Bake covered for 30-35 minutes at 350° F.

Minimizing Your Risk (page 2)

- Breastfeed your baby. Breastfeeding seems to offer some women protection against breast cancer and it's good for the baby. Breastfeed for at least four months.

- Quit smoking. Smoking tobacco and breathing second-hand smoke have been linked to breast cancer. Tobacco smoke is linked to 30 per cent of all cancer deaths.

- Weigh the risks and benefits of taking birth control pills. Taking birth controls pills may slightly increase your risk of breast cancer if you are a long term pill user and began taking birth control pills at a young age. Since birth control pills also offer benefits, discuss this with your doctor.

- Talk to your doctor about the risks and benefits of hormone replacement therapy (HRT). HRT can relieve symptoms of menopause. Using HRT for a long time may increase your risk of breast cancer.

- Limit your exposure to pesticides and other potentially harmful chemicals.

Health Canada, November 2002, Reproduced with the permission of the Minister of Public Works and Government Services Canada, 2004.

Desserts

"A compromise is the art of dividing a cake in such a way that everyone believes that he has got the biggest piece."   Ludwig Erhard

ALMOND CUBES WITH FRUIT

3 envelopes unflavored gelatin

1 cup sugar

4 cups cold water

1 cup milk

1 tablespoon almond extract

½ cup maraschino cherries

1 -20 ounce can pineapple chunks, chilled

1 -11 ounce can mandarin orange sections, chilled

In a large saucepan combine unflavored gelatin
and sugar; stir in 2 cups of the cold water.
Cook and stir over low heat till gelatin and sugar
are dissolved. Remove from heat; stir in
remaining cold water, milk and almond extract.
Pour into a 9 x 13 inch pan. Chill until firm.
Cut gelatin into small cubes. Rinse and drain
cherries. Mix very gently into the gelatin cubes;
the cherries, undrained pineapple chunks, and
undrained mandarin orange sections. Serve as a
fruit bowl with brunch or as a lunch dessert.
Serves 12.

APPLE & CHEDDAR CHEESE CRISP

6 cups pared sliced apples

1 teaspoon cinnamon

1 tablespoon lemon juice

½ cup corn syrup

½ cup sugar

⅔ cup all-purpose flour

¼ teaspoon salt

⅓ cup butter

1 cup grated cheddar cheese

Arrange the apples in a greased 10 x 6 x 2 inch baking dish. Sprinkle with cinnamon and pour lemon juice and corn syrup over. Combine sugar, flour and salt. Cut in butter until mixture is the consistency of cornmeal. Gently mix in cheese. Sprinkle this mixture over the apples. Bake in a 350° F. oven for 1 hour or until the apples are tender. Serves 4 to 6.

APPLE CRISP

6 cups sliced apples

¼ cup white sugar

2 tablespoons lemon juice

¾ cup rolled oats

½ cup brown sugar

½ cup flour

1 teaspoon cinnamon

⅓ cup butter or margarine

Whipped cream or ice cream for garnish.

Arrange apples in a buttered 2-quart ovenproof casserole. Sprinkle apples with white sugar and lemon juice. Combine rolled oats, sugar, flour and cinnamon. Cut in butter until mixture is crumbly and sprinkle over apples. Bake at 350°F for 40 minutes or until apples are tender. Serve warm with whipped cream or ice cream. You can substitute chopped rhubarb, blueberries or saskatoons for the sliced apples. Serves 6.

"Worry is like a rocking chair: It gives you something to do, but it doesn't get you anywhere."

Erma Bombeck

APPLE PANDOWDY

1 cup flour
2 tablespoons butter
2 teaspoons baking powder
¼ teaspoon salt
1 teaspoon sugar
½ cup milk
Mix to make a soft dough.
Roll dough rather thin.
Spread:
1 ½ cups apples — finely chopped
½ cup brown sugar
sprinkle nutmeg
Place a few dollops of butter over this. Roll up as you would a jelly roll. Cut in one inch slices. Place in greased baking pan.
Sauce:
½ cup sugar
1 tablespoon flour
pinch of salt
Put in small saucepan over medium heat. Gradually pour 1 cup of boiling water over the sauce. Stir until thickened and add two tablespoons butter. Pour over apple rolls in pan. Bake at 350° F. for about 30 minutes or until light brown.

THE "BREAST" CHEESECAKE

Graham Wafer Crust:
2 cups graham wafers, crushed
¼ cup margarine, melted
¼ cup sugar
Mix and press into 9 inch springform pan.

Filling:
2 -8 ounce packages cream cheese, softened
3 eggs
¾ cup white sugar
2 cups sour cream
2 teaspoons vanilla
Combine eggs and sugar and beat until sugar is
dissolved. Beat in cream cheese. Add sour cream and
vanilla and mix in. Pour into prepared springform pan.
Bake in a 350°F. oven for 60 minutes. Cool to
room temperature. Chill for 24 hours in the
refrigerator. To serve top with whipped cream and
seasonal fresh fruit.

BANANA PINEAPPLE CHEESECAKE SQUARE

2 cups graham wafer crumbs

⅓ cup margarine, melted

¼ cup sugar

3 packages cream cheese, softened

¾ cup sugar

1 teaspoon vanilla

3 eggs

½ cup ripe bananas, mashed

1 banana, sliced

1 teaspoon lemon juice

1 cup strawberries, halved

1 -8 ounce can pineapple chunks, drained

sprinkle pecans, chopped (optional)

4-ounces semi-sweet baking chocolate, melted

Mix crumbs, melted margarine and sugar. Press into 9 x 13 inch pan. Mix cream cheese, sugar and vanilla with electric mixer. Add eggs and mix until blended. Stir in bananas. Pour over crust. Bake at 350° F. for 30 minutes. Chill for at least 3 hours. Toss banana with lemon juice. Mix in strawberries and pineapple. Spoon evenly over cheesecake. Sprinkle with nuts and melted chocolate. Cut into squares.

CHOCOLATE TOFFEE DESSERT

½ cup butter, softened
2 cups icing sugar
2-3 tablespoons cocoa
2 eggs, separated
Dash of salt
1 package (100 gram) sliced almonds, toasted
1 teaspoon vanilla
1 cup vanilla wafers, crushed

Cream butter, icing sugar, cocoa and salt. Add egg yolks one at a time, beat until mixture is creamy. Stir in almonds and vanilla.
Beat egg whites just until stiff; fold into above mixture. Spread half of crumbs in bottom of 8 inch square pan. Spoon on cocoa mixture. Top with remaining crumbs. Refrigerate overnight to mellow. At serving time, cut into small squares; top with whipped cream. Serves 9.

In 1974 I wanted to move to California because it's cool. In 2004 I want to move to California because it's warm.

CARROT PUDDING
AND RUM SAUCE

(Christmas would not be the same without
the traditional Christmas pudding.)

1 ½ cups grated carrots   1 ½ cups grated apples

1 ½ cups grated potatoes   ¾ cup melted butter

1 ½ cup brown sugar   3 cups raisins

1 ½ cups flour   1 ½ teaspoons nutmeg

1 ½ teaspoons cinnamon   1 ½ teaspoons salt

1 ½ teaspoons baking soda   1 ½ tablespoons lemon juice

Combine the above ingredients in a large bowl until
thoroughly mixed. If you have a canner and sealers,
spoon batter into one quart jars, filling only to ¾ full.
Seal. Place in water bath in canner. Boil for three
hours.
* If you are not equipped for canning, divide pudding
into oven safe bowls or tube pans. Cover them and place
them in a deep pan of boiling water in the oven. Water
should be half way up the side of the pudding containers.
Steam in 350° F. oven for 3 to 4 hours, adding more
water as required. To serve — heat and serve with rum
sauce. Rum Sauce on next page.................

250

RUM SAUCE

½ cup butter

¾ cup brown sugar

¼ cup cream

½ teaspoon rum extract or 2 tablespoons rum

Melt butter in saucepan, add brown sugar, mix well and boil for 2 minutes. Add cream and boil for 2 minutes longer. Remove from heat. Add rum flavoring.

CHOCOLATE FONDUE

(A great dessert that can be served later in
the evening as a help yourself.)

½ cup white sugar	¼ cup unsweetened cocoa
1 tablespoon cornstarch	¾ cup whole milk
1 tablespoon butter	1 teaspoon orange extract

1 tablespoon Amaretto or Frangelico liqueur (optional)

In a small saucepan, mix sugar, cocoa and cornstarch. Whisk in milk. Cook on low, stirring constantly until mixture boils and thickens. Remove from heat. Blend in butter, extract and liqueur. Transfer to a fondue pot or heated slow cooker. Serve with fresh chunky fruit, biscotti, shortbread, cubed pound cake or marshmallows.

CLASSIC CRÈME CARAMEL

1 cup sugar (divided into 2)   2 cups milk

1 cup heavy cream   ¼ teaspoon salt

4 eggs and 2 additional egg yolks

2 teaspoons vanilla extract

Preheat the oven to 325° F. Butter 8 ramekins or -6 ounce custard cups. In small skillet over medium heat, melt ½ cup sugar stirring constantly until it becomes a light brown syrup. Divide the hot caramel syrup among the 8 ramekins. Place cups in shallow baking pan. In a large bowl with mixer at low speed beat eggs and egg yolks, salt and ½ cup sugar until lemon colored. Gradually beat in milk, cream and vanilla. Strain though a sieve into the ramekins on top of the caramel syrup. Carefully pour boiling water into the baking dish until ⅔ of the way up the sides of the ramekins. (Be careful not to get any water on the custard mixture.) Bake 1 hour or until inserted knife comes out clean. Cool on wire racks and then chill in the refrigerator. Loosen custard from cups and invert onto dessert dishes, letting syrup run over custard and down sides onto the dish.

REFRESHING LIME PIE
(A light hot day dessert!)

1 -9 inch prepared graham wafer crust

1 -3 ounce box lime flavored gelatin, sugar free

½ cup boiling water

2 cups light lime yogurt

2 cups frozen light whipped topping, thawed

In large bowl, dissolve gelatin in boiling water. With wire whisk, stir in yogurt. Fold in whipped topping and transfer to prepared crust. Refrigerate until set.

GRANDMA'S RASPBERRY PIE

1 -3 ounce package raspberry jello powder

¾ cup sugar

2 ½ tablespoons corn starch

1 ¾ cup water

2 tablespoons butter

4 cups raspberries

1 -9 inch baked piecrust

Bring water to a boil in a large pot. Mix dry ingredients together and add to the water-stirring occasionally. Cook on medium heat until thick, approximately 10 minutes. Add butter and let cool. Add berries and pour into piecrust. Chill and serve with whipped cream.

CRUNCHY FROZEN DESSERT

(This is so delicious. A great dessert for summer get-togethers. Because it is a frozen dessert it can be made a few days ahead of the event.)

Base:

1 ½ cups vanilla wafer crumbs

½ cup chopped peanuts

¼ cup melted butter

2 tablespoons peanut butter

Mix all together, remove 1 cup to use for topping and pat remaining crumbs in buttered 9 x 13 inch pan.

Second layer:

1 -8 ounce package cream cheese

½ cup sugar

3 eggs

2 tablespoons vanilla

½ cup peanut butter

1 large tub cool whip

Beat cheese, sugar, eggs, vanilla and peanut butter till smooth. Mix in cool whip and spread on base. Sprinkle with crumbs left over from base. Freeze in deep freeze and remove one hour before serving.

EASY POLYNESIAN
WEDDING DESSERT

(This starts with a mix and is so easy, yet makes
a dessert fit for company or a Polynesian wedding!)

1 yellow cake mix
3 eggs
½ cup oil
1 can mandarin oranges with juice
Mix together – spread in a greased 9 x 13 inch pan
and bake according to mix directions. Let cool.
Topping
1 large tub of cool whip
1 can crushed pineapple
1 vanilla instant pudding
Mix cool whip, crushed pineapple with juice and dry
pudding powder together and spread on top of cool cake.
Let sit for a few hours before serving. (Better if left
overnight.)

*"Though it sounds absurd, it is true to say I felt
younger at sixty than I felt at twenty."* Ellen Glasgow

DOUBLE LEMON CHEESECAKE

1 cup vanilla wafer cookie crumbs

3 tablespoons sugar

3 tablespoons margarine, melted

3 -8 ounce packages, cream cheese, softened

1 cup sugar

3 tablespoons flour

2 tablespoons lemon juice

1 tablespoon lemon peel, grated

½ teaspoon vanilla

3 eggs

1 egg white

¾ cup sugar

2 tablespoons cornstarch

½ cup water

¼ cup lemon juice

1 egg yolk, beaten

Mix crumbs, sugar and butter and press into a
9-inch spring form pan. Bake in 325° F. oven
for 10 minutes. Mix cream cheese, sugar, flour,
juice, lemon peel and vanilla with electric mixer
until well blended. Add 3 eggs and egg white,
Continued on next page...............

DOUBLE LEMON CHEESECAKE continued..

mixing on low until blended. Pour over crust and bake in 325° F. oven for 50-55 minutes. Refrigerate for at least 3 hours. In saucepan combine sugar and cornstarch. Gradually stir in water and juice. Bring mixture to low boil on medium heat; stirring constantly until clear and thickened. Stir in 2 tablespoons of the hot mixture into egg yolks and return to hot mixture. Cook about 1 minute or until thickened. Cool slightly and spoon over cheesecake. Refrigerate.

IMPOSSIBLE PIE!
(An awesome quick dessert!)

4 eggs	¼ cup margarine, melted
½ cup flour	2 cups whole milk
1 cup sugar	1 cup coconut
2 teaspoons vanilla	¼ teaspoon salt
½ teaspoon baking powder	

Blend all together in blender for a few seconds until well mixed. Pour into greased 10 inch pie plate. Bake at 350° F. about 45 minutes, until center tests firm. Flour will settle to form crust, coconut forms topping and center is an egg custard.

FRESH PINEAPPLE WITH CARAMEL DIPPING SAUCE

Skewers of fresh pineapple pieces
1 cup brown sugar
1 tablespoon corn syrup
1/4 cup water
3/4 cup whipping cream
1 tablespoons butter
2 teaspoons vanilla

Bring sugar, corn syrup, and water to a boil over high heat in a covered heavy saucepan. Simmer for 3 to 4 minutes. Remove from heat and slowly whisk in cream (watch out for steam). Stir in butter and vanilla. Let cool for 20 minutes before serving. Have two or three dishes of caramel sauce on the table so they can be easily reached by all. Dip the skewered pineapple into the caramel sauce for a delicious, sweet ending to a good meal.
* Leftover caramels make a delicious caramel sauce for this dish too — just melt caramels in a heavy pot with a few tablespoons of water and when they are completely melted add enough heavy cream so they will stay creamy and not harden again when they cool.

FRIED BANANAS IN RUM CREAM

4 medium bananas, peeled
2 tablespoons butter
¼ cup rum cream liqueur (or any favorite creamed
liqueur that goes with bananas)
2 tablespoons brown sugar
½ cup heavy cream

Have dessert dishes prepared with a scoop of vanilla ice
cream. Cut bananas in half lengthwise and place in a
hot skillet. After 30 seconds pour rum creme liqueur
over the bananas. Lower heat to medium and sauté for 1
to 2 minutes, flipping the bananas over often. Sprinkle
bananas with brown sugar and let the sugar melt. Pour
cream over bananas and let simmer for another minute.
Serve over ice cream immediately.

*"Mid-life brings with it an appreciation for what is
important. We realize that breasts sag, hips expand and
chins double, but our loved ones make the journey
worthwhile. Would any of you trade the knowledge that
you have now, for the body you had way back when?
Maybe our bodies simply have to expand to hold all the
wisdom and love we've acquired. That's my reasoning and
I'm sticking to it!" Unknown*

LAST MINUTE
SCRUMPTIOUS DESSERT
(Every one needs a recipe that takes 10 minutes
and it's good to go - wherever it is you have to take it!)

2 cups vanilla flavoured yogurt
1 package vanilla instant pudding
1 package Cool Whip
1 can of prepared pie filling of your choice
Graham Wafers

Line 9 x 13 pan with graham wafers. Combine
yogurt, pudding, and Cool Whip and pour over
graham wafers. Spread with your favorite pie filling.
Chill and serve with whipped cream.

If you're a bear, you get to hibernate. You do
nothing but sleep for six months.
I could deal with that.
Before you hibernate, you're supposed to eat
yourself stupid. I could deal with that, too.
If you're a mama bear, everyone knows you mean
business. You swat anyone who bothers your cubs.
If your cubs get out of line, you swat them too.
Your husband expects you to growl when you
wake up. He also expects you to have hairy legs
and excess body fat.
Sometimes, I wish I was a bear!

LEMON DESSERT

1st layer: 2 cups flour

               1 cup margarine

               1 cup chopped pecans

Soften margarine. Add flour and pecans. Press into two 8 inch springform pans. Bake at 350°F. for 15 minutes. Cool.

2nd layer: 2 -8 ounce packages cream cheese

               1 cup icing sugar

               1 cup whipping cream (whipped)

Beat cream cheese and icing sugar and add whipped cream.

3rd layer: 2 packages lemon pie filling (cooked according to package and cooled).

4th layer: 2 cups whipping cream

               ½ cup sugar

               1 teaspoon vanilla

Whip cream and add sugar and vanilla.

Garnish with slivered almonds.

MAMMA'S BREAD PUDDING

Heat to scalding 2 cups milk
Place 4 cups coarse bite size pieces of dry bread in
buttered baking pan.
Pour hot milk over bread.
Cool slightly then distribute over bread mixture:
1 ½ cups frozen saskatoons (or fresh fruit in season) or
1 can of peaches (sliced and drained).
Mix together well: ¼ cup melted butter
                    2 eggs slightly beaten
                    1 teaspoon nutmeg
                    ½ cup sugar
                    ⅛ teaspoon salt
Pour evenly over ingredients in pan.
Bake at 350° F. for about 35 minutes or until golden
brown and custard is firm. Awesome served warm with
cream, ice cream or vanilla sauce.
Vanilla Sauce
3 egg yolks   ½ cup sugar
1 ½ teaspoons vanilla   1cup heavy cream
In a small bowl combine sugar and egg yolks. In a
saucepan heat cream and when hot add small amount to
egg yolks and sugar to heat them. Then add back into
the saucepan with the remaining cream and simmer until
thick stirring constantly. Do not boil. Strain and chill.

MINI CHOCOLATE SOUFFLES
(You'll feel like a chef when you serve these.)

1 cup sugar — divided for use 3 times in recipe

¼ cup all purpose flour

1 ¼ cups milk

3 squares unsweetened chocolate

5 eggs — separated

¼ teaspoon salt

1 ½ teaspoons vanilla extract

1 cup heavy cream, whipped

Preheat oven to 350° F. Grease 6 – 10 ounce custard cups or soufflé dishes. Sprinkle each one lightly with sugar (using approximately ¼ cup). In saucepan combine flour and ¼ cup sugar, gradually add milk and cook over medium heat until smooth and thickened. Remove from heat. Stir chocolate into mixture until melted. Beat in egg yolks all together until well mixed. Set aside and cool till lukewarm. In large bowl at high speed, beat egg whites, salt and vanilla. When peaks form add sugar slowly until whites are very stiff. Gently fold chocolate mixture into beaten egg whites until blended and spoon into custard cups. Place cups into a baking pan and bake for 30 to 35 minutes until puffy and starting to brown. Place a dollop of whipped cream and a drizzle of the delicious fudge sauce featured on page 279 or a commercial chocolate sundae sauce works too.

PAVLOVA

4 egg whites, at room temperature
¼ teaspoon salt
1 teaspoon vanilla
1 teaspoon vinegar
1 cup sugar
1 tablespoon cornstarch

Line cookie sheet with greased foil. Draw a 10 inch circle on the foil.
Beat egg whites and salt until peaks form, but not dry. Add vanilla and vinegar and beat well. Mix sugar and cornstarch together in a small bowl. Add 1 tablespoon at a time to egg whites beating well after each addition.
Spread meringue inside circle on paper — building it up around the edge. Bake at 275° F. for 1 hour. Turn oven off and leave meringue in oven to dry for 1 hour. Serve with whipped cream and fresh fruit.

"I know for sure that what we dwell on is who we become." Oprah Winfrey

PECAN PIE
(Delicious!!)

Pastry:

Mix the following with a pastry blender:

1 pound lard

1 pound margarine

9 cups flour

2 teaspoons baking powder

3 tablespoons brown sugar

Mix and add to above mixture:

1 cup cold water

2 eggs

2 tablespoons vinegar

This pastry is so easy to work with. Freeze it in portions, thaw and roll as needed. Roll on well floured surface.

Filling:

1 cup corn syrup	1 cup brown sugar
3 eggs	⅓ cup butter
1 teaspoon vanilla	1 cup pecans
pinch of salt	

Mix all ingredients and pour into unbaked pie shell.

Bake at 350° F. for 45 minutes.

Serve with whipped cream or ice cream.

MOCHA MUD PIE

(Not difficult but there are many stages that must be started hours before serving. Once mastered, this dessert becomes a legend- the serving sizes are mammoth and delicious.)

1 ⅓ cups of chocolate wafer crumbs
⅓ cup butter or margarine
5 to 7 cups of vanilla ice cream (depending on the shape of the bowl that you use)
2 tablespoons instant coffee (you can adjust to taste)
½ cup cocoa
4 tablespoons butter
1 cup sugar (divided)
1 ½ cups whipping cream (divided)

Crust: Melt butter and mix with crumbs. Press into a 9 inch pie plate. Bake at 375°F for 10-12 minutes. Remove from oven and cool.

Filling: Find a flat bottomed bowl with the same size rim as your pie plate. (just slightly smaller works even better) Fold 2 tablespoons instant coffee (dissolved in 1 – 1½ tablespoons of hot water) into the ice cream. Put

Continued on next page..............

Shown on previous page:

- Lemon Dessert... page 261
- Devil's Food Cake with Mocha Icing...page 302 and 303
- Orange Cake with Creamy White Frosting... page 313 and 314
- Schmoo Torte... page 286

MOCHA MUD PIE continued.............

the coffee ice cream into the bowl, and into the freezer for a few hours and let it set well.

Prepare fudge sauce: In large saucepan over medium heat- mix cocoa, ¾ cup sugar, butter and ½ cup cream. Bring mixture to a full rolling boil, remove from heat and add vanilla. Cool.

To assemble: when crust is cool and ice cream has been set quite hard....dip bowl quickly into a sink of hot water to unmold the ice cream- be careful not to let any water get into the ice cream. Turn the bowl over onto the pie plate so the mound of ice cream falls onto the chocolate crust. If the mound of ice cream has a flat top — great — if not you may want to cut a little of the ice cream away so the top of the mound is flat. Pour chocolate syrup over the top and let it drizzle down the sides. Place back into the freezer to set hard. You may have to do this in stages so the fudge stays on the ice cream. If you have more chocolate sauce than will stay on the ice cream- save some for later. When the chocolate covered dome has frozen hard, whip the remaining cream (1 cup) with the remaining sugar (¼ cup) till stiff and spread whipped cream over all. This may be garnished with grated chocolate. Cut into wedges with a hot knife, serve and wait for the compliments.

PINA COLADA CHEESECAKE

Crust:　1 cup graham crumbs
　　　　3 tablespoons brown sugar
　　　　¼ cup butter
Mix together and press into a 9-inch springform pan.
Bake at 400 F for 5 minutes.

Filling:　2 envelopes gelatin
　　　　　¼ cup coconut rum
　　　　　1 can (19 ounce) crushed pineapple, drained
　　　　　⅓ cup sugar
　　　　　pinch of salt
　　　　　1 egg
　　　　　8 ounce package cream cheese
　　　　　¾ cup whipping cream

Filling:　Sprinkle gelatin over rum to soften. Combine
pineapple, sugar, salt, and egg in saucepan. Stir in
softened gelatin and heat. Stir until thickened. Remove
from heat and cool. Beat cream cheese and whipped
cream until smooth. Add to pineapple mixture. Beat
for 2 minutes. Pour over crust and chill for 4 hours.

PMS CHOCOLATE TRIFLE

(It may not cure PMS but it sure makes the
suffering easier to take.)

6 chocolate bars (Skor or Crispy Crunch-pick your
favorite)

4 packages chocolate mouse

2 large tubs of Cool Whip

1 chocolate cake mix

½ cup Kalhua or chocolate sauce

Bake cake, cut into squares and place in bowl, pour ½
cup of chocolate sauce or Kalhua over cake, cover and
let sit overnight in the refrigerator. Freeze the chocolate
bars. Next day - beat the mousse according to package
directions. Crush the chocolate bars. Put ½ of the
squares of cake in the bottom of a large bowl, cover with
1 tub of cool whip and then half of the mousse and
sprinkle half of the crushed chocolate bars over. Start
again with the cake and repeat layers.

Some days don't you just want to add chocolate to
everything — even the cheese omelet! This dessert is a
sure cure.

**There are four basic food groups, milk
chocolate, dark chocolate, white chocolate, and
chocolate truffles.**

PEANUT BUTTER LOVER'S PIE

1 -9 inch pastry shell (prepared or your own)
1 -8 ounce package cream cheese
1 cup peanut butter, smooth or crunchy
1¼ cups icing sugar
½ cup whipping cream
2 teaspoons vanilla
½ cup whipping cream
6 - 1-ounce squares semi-sweet chocolate,
coarsely chopped

Preheat oven to 400° F. Prick pie shell and
bake for 10-minutes. In large mixing bowl, beat
cream cheese. Add peanut butter and 1 cup of
the icing sugar. Beat until well blended. In
small bowl, using an electric mixer, beat ½ cup
whipping cream until peaks form. Gradually
add the remaining ½ cup of icing sugar and
vanilla. Gently fold in ½ of the whipped cream
mixture into the peanut butter mixture. Mix until
just blended and add remaining cream mixture.
Continued on next page.................

Pour mixture into the baked, cooled pie shell and smooth top. For the topping; microwave ½ cup whipping cream with chocolate from 2-3 minutes on medium power. Stir occasionally. You can also heat in saucepan on stove for about 5 minutes. Stir until chocolate is melted and mixture is smooth. Cool until lukewarm and pour over cooled pie. Refrigerate, uncovered, until topping is firm. Cover with plastic wrap once topping is set. This pie freezes well or keep in the refrigerator for 2 days.

"Beginning today, treat everyone you meet as if they were going to be dead by midnight. Extend them all the care, kindness and understanding you can muster. Your life will never be the same again." Og Mandino

POPPY SEED DESSERT

(A light, not too sweet dessert)

Crust: ½ cup wafer crumbs

½ cup flour

½ cup margarine

Mix and press into 9 inch square pan. Bake in 350° F. oven for 10 minutes.

Filling: 1 cup sugar

3 tablespoons cornstarch

3 egg yolks

½ cup poppy seeds

1 tablespoon (1 package) gelatin

¼ cup cold water

2 cups milk

1 teaspoon vanilla

3 egg whites

¼ cup sugar

¼ teaspoon cream of tartar

Mix sugar, cornstarch, egg yolks and poppy seeds. Dissolve gelatin in water and milk and add to poppyseed mixture. Bring to a boil. Remove from heat and add vanilla. Cool slightly. Beat egg whites, sugar and cream of tartar. Fold into cooked, cooled mixture. Spread over baked crust. Cover with whipped topping.

*Serve with Saskatoon Sauce or any fruit or pie filling.

PUMPKIN CHIFFON PIE

1 baked 9-inch pie crust
1 envelope unflavored gelatin (1 tablespoon)
½ cup brown sugar
½ teaspoon salt
½ teaspoon cinnamon
½ teaspoon nutmeg
½ teaspoon ginger
⅛ teaspoon cloves
1 ¼ cups pumpkin
3 egg yolks
½ cup milk
¼ teaspoon cream of tartar
3 eggs whites
½ cup brown sugar
Mix gelatin, ½ cup of the brown sugar, salt and
spices. Beat in pumpkin, egg yolks and milk.
Bring to a boil in a saucepan, over medium heat,
stirring constantly. Chill until slightly thickened,
stirring occasionally. Beat egg whites and cream
of tartar until soft peaks form. Gradually beat in
remaining ½ cup brown sugar, until stiff. Fold
into pumpkin mixture, pour into baked pie shell
and chill until firm. (About 3 hours.)

PRALINE CHEESECAKE

(This cheesecake will keep nicely in the fridge for two days or it freezes well.)

Base:

1 cup flour

¼ cup brown sugar

¼ cup unsalted butter, softened

¼ cup pecans, coarsely chopped

Beat butter, brown sugar and flour. Stir in pecans, Press mixture into a greased 9 inch spring form pan. Bake at 350° F. for 10 minutes and cool.

Cheesecake:

3 -8 ounce packages cream cheese, softened

¾ cup white sugar

2 tablespoons flour

3 eggs

1 cup sour cream

⅓ cup maple syrup

⅓ cup pecans, chopped

Beat cream cheese, sugar and flour until smooth. Beat in eggs, one at a time and add the sour cream. Mix in maple syrup and pecans. Pour over base and bake in 375°F oven for about 45- 50 minutes. Continued on next page...

PRALINE CHEESECAKE continued.....
Turn oven off and let cake stand in oven for 2-hours.

Topping:

¾ cup corn syrup	1½ cups pecan halves
1½ cups brown sugar	¼ cup butter

In saucepan melt butter: add corn syrup, brown sugar and pecans. Let mixture come to boil and boil for 3-minutes. Mixture should be thick but pourable. If too thick, add 1 tablespoon of water. Pour over cheesecake and spread evenly. Refrigerate until chilled.

POLYNESIAN PINEAPPLE FLAMBE

¼ cup white sugar	¼ cup rum
¼ cup cream	

2 cups pineapple – fresh spears or canned chunks or rings

1 tablespoon lemon juice	1 teaspoon vanilla

2 tablespoons macadamia nuts

pinch of salt

Put white sugar into a sauté pan and stir until melted and golden brown. Add rum and cream. Add pineapple. Simmer for 1 minute. Add lemon juice and vanilla. Add macadamia nuts and salt. Delicious served over vanilla ice cream balls.

PUMPKIN TORTE

2 cups graham wafer crumbs

⅓ cup sugar

½ cup, plus 2 tablespoons melted margarine

1- 8-ounce package cream cheese, softened

¾ cup sugar

2 eggs

2 cups pumpkin

½ cup milk

3 eggs, separated

½ cup sugar

1 teaspoon cinnamon

2 envelopes gelatin, unflavored

¼ cup water

Mix together graham wafers, sugar and melted margarine. Press into an 8x10-inch pan. Beat together cream cheese, sugar and eggs and pour over graham crumb base. Bring to a boil; pumpkin, milk, egg yolks, sugar and cinnamon. Add gelatin, soaked in ¼ cup water. Remove from heat. Cool well. Beat egg whites, fold in cooled pumpkin, and then pour over crust and cream cheese. Let set well; top off with whipped cream.

RHUBARB MERINGUE TORTE
(This recipe is easily doubled for a 9 x 13 pan.)

CRUST:
1 cup flour
2 tablespoons sugar
⅛ teaspoon salt
½ cup butter or margarine
Blend until crumbly. Press into a 9 x 9 inch
pan. Bake 20 minutes at 325° F.

FILLING:
3 tablespoons flour
1 ¼ cups sugar
3 cups rhubarb, chopped
⅛ teaspoon salt
3 egg yolks
½ cup evaporated milk or cream
Cook together and stir until thick. Pour over
baked crust and top with meringue.
3 egg whites
3 tablespoons sugar
½ teaspoon vanilla
Brown under broiler or bake 15 minutes at
350° F.

RHUBARB SENSATION

2 cups of flour
½ cup margarine
¼ teaspoon salt
1 teaspoon baking powder
1 egg (beaten)

Mix and rub into crumbs. Save ¾ cup for topping and press the rest into a 9 x 13 cake pan.

Mix together:
4 cups rhubarb cut into ½ inch pieces.
1½ cups sugar
½ cup flour
2 eggs (lightly beaten)

Put on top of crumb layer and cover with ¾ cup crumbs. Sprinkle some cinnamon and sugar on crumbs Bake at 325° for 1 hour. Serve warm with whipped cream or ice cream.   Freezes well.

"Women and cats will do as they please, and men and dogs should relax and get used to the idea."
Robert A. Heinlein

RICH CREAMY HOT FUDGE SAUCE
(Also good over crepes, soufflés,
ice cream, or fresh fruit.)

2 tablespoons cocoa powder

1 cup sugar

1 cup heavy cream

1 tablespoon corn syrup or golden syrup

½ teaspoon vanilla

1 tablespoon butter

In a saucepan, blend cocoa, sugar, syrup and heavy cream over medium heat and bring to a boil. Simmer for 5 minutes. Remove from heat and add vanilla and butter. Best served hot.

"You don't just luck into things as much as you'd like to think you do. You build step by step, whether it's friendships or opportunities."

Barbara Bush

ROSEBUSH STRAWBERRY PIE

Crust:
1 cup flour
½ cup margarine
2 tablespoons icing sugar
Pinch of salt

Sift together flour, icing sugar and salt. Cut the margarine into these ingredients with a pastry blender. Blend well. Pat or roll out into a 9-inch pie plate. Bake at 350°F. for 15 minutes.

STRAWBERRY FILLING:
1 small package strawberry jello
½ cup sugar
¾ cup water
2 tablespoons cornstarch
1 quart strawberries, sliced

In a small saucepan, cook cornstarch, water and sugar until clear and thick. Remove from heat, add jello powder (dry); mix. Add strawberries. Pour into the baked pie shell. Chill. Garnish with whipped cream.

SAGO PUDDING

(This is a traditional slow cooking stove top hot pudding.
Lovely to prepare during the long, cold prairie winters.
A large recipe it keeps well in the fridge.)

2 ½ quarts (10 to 13 cups) boiling water (10 cups will make a thick pudding — 13 thinner)

25 prunes (pitted)

1 ½ cups raisins

Boil, then simmer until fruit is plump, about 45 minutes

Add: 1¼ cups sago (Stir, watching carefully as this sticks easily and cook for awhile)

Add: 1 cup sugar

    1 teaspoon salt

    1 teaspoon cinnamon mixed with 2 tablespoons sugar

    1 teaspoon vinegar

After each addition, cook awhile before adding another.
After adding vinegar, cook until sago is clear. Can be quite thin while hot.

What the heck is Sago? It is in your grocery store with the tapioca....it looks like little white marbles...it is actually starch extracted from the sago (and other tropical) palms that is processed into flour, meal and pearl sago, which is similar to tapioca. South Pacific cooks frequently use sago for baking and for thickening soups, puddings and other desserts. Try it — it's great!

SASKATCHEWAN SASKATOON PIE

Saskatoon filling:

1 ¼ cups water

1 cup sugar

2 tablespoons lemon juice

5 cups saskatoon berries

2 tablespoons cornstarch

1- 2 tablespoons butter

In a saucepan, boil water and sugar together with lemon juice. Add saskatoon berries and cook for 15 minutes over medium heat. Do not cook longer as this makes the berries tough. In a cup combine cornstarch with 3 tablespoons water to make a smooth paste. Pour into cooked berry juice and cook until thickened, stirring as necessary. Remove from heat. Stir in the butter. Pour into into an uncooked 9-inch pie shell.   Cover with second crust or lattice pastry strips. Bake at 450° F. for 10 minutes. Reduce to 350° F. and cook for 35 minutes.

SASKATOON BERRY SAUCE
(Great on pancakes, ice cream or cake.)

2 cups Saskatoons

1 cup water

2 tablespoons cornstarch

¾ cup sugar

juice from 1 lemon

Place Saskatoons in saucepan with water and bring to a boil. Simmer 5 minutes. Blend cornstarch and sugar, add slowly to Saskatoons. Simmer until thick and clear, around 15 minutes. Add lemon juice and cool.

Laughter can be good for your health
Stress can affect not only your outlook but how you feel physically. Some feel stress increases your chances for diseases from cancer to heart problems to stroke. Reducing stress can greatly improve your quality of life so anything that helps relieve stress is a plus. Laughter is a great way to let off steam and have a good time. Whether it's watching a funny movie, or enjoying friends, laughter can make you feel better and maybe even live longer.

SASKATOON CRISP

4 cups fresh or frozen Saskatoons
1 tablespoon lemon juice
2 tablespoon water
1 cup sugar
1 – 2 tablespoons minute tapioca (depending on how
juicy the berries are)
1 tablespoon butter

Simmer berries, water and lemon juice for about 10
minutes. Add sugar and tapioca and then spread into a
9 X 13 inch baking pan. Dot with butter and top with
the following:
1 ¼ cups quick cooking rolled oats
¾ cup brown sugar
1 cup flour
½ cup margarine
Combine oats, sugar and flour and cut in butter.
Sprinkle mixture over berries and bake at 350° F for
25 – 30 minutes. Serve warm or cold with ice cream
or whipped cream.
*Note: This is delicious if you add raspberries or cut
up apples to Saskatoons.

SCRUMPTIOUS TIRAMISU

1 -6 ounce package of jello vanilla cooked
pudding
1 -8 ounce package cream cheese
¼ cup coffee liqueur
1 tablespoon instant coffee
½ cup hot water
1 tablespoon sugar
1 -8 ounce package lady fingers
1 ½ cups Cool Whip, thawed
4 squares semi-sweet chocolate, coarsely grated

Prepare pudding as per package. Whisk cream
cheese and liqueur into hot pie filling. Cover
with plastic wrap and chill 1 hour. Combine
coffee, hot water and sugar; brush over lady
fingers. Fold whipped topping into pudding
mixture. Line bottom of 8 cup trifle bowl with
half of the lady fingers. Spread half of pudding
mixture over fingers; sprinkle with half of the
grated chocolate. Repeat layers. Cover tightly
with plastic wrap and chill at least 4 hours or
overnight to blend flavors. Serves 10 – 12.

SCHMOO TORTE

(Don't be alone with this- people have been known to eat the entire trifle!!!)

Cake:

7 eggs and 1 egg white

1 cup sugar (divided in half)

½ cup cake flour (sifted one time)

1 heaping teaspoon baking powder

¼ teaspoon cream of tartar

1 teaspoon vanilla

Separate whites and yolks. Beat egg yolks and add ½ cup sugar and 1 teaspoon vanilla.

Beat egg whites until almost stiff and add cream of tartar and ½ cup sugar. Fold egg yolks into whites, then fold in flour and baking powder. Use wooden spoon. Add nuts. Bake in 350° F. oven for one hour in 9 inch angel food pan. Take out of oven and cool. When completely cool, slice into 3 sections. Freeze layers with wax paper between each layer.

To Decorate: Do the night before or in the morning. Whip 3 pints of whipping cream with 10 tablespoons of sifted icing sugar and 1 teaspoon of vanilla.

Sauce:

½ pint whipping cream

1 ½ cups brown sugar

1 heaping tablespoon butter ...continued on next page.

Pour whipping cream in saucepan, stir in sugar and butter. Bring to a gentle boil and boil for 1 minute. Let cool and put in refrigerator. When icing and sauce are ready, take cake out of freezer.

Place first layer of cake on large plate and top with whipping cream. Spoon sauce over cream layer. Continue on all layers except top.

Top layer: Cover sides and top of cake with whipping cream. Drizzle sauce over top. Put remaining cream around base of cake and pipe around hole in center. Take whole pecans and stand in rows along the sides of the cake. Use additional sauce to spoon over each serving.

Note: This recipe also works well as a trifle.
- Cut the cake into cubes and place a layer of cake in the bottom of a trifle bowl.
- Spoon cream mixture over cake.
- Spread sauce over cream mixture.
- Sprinkle chopped pecans over sauce.

Continue to layer until trifle bowl is full.

SOUR CREAM & RAISIN PIE
(A Family Favorite — Don't even think about counting the calories in this one!)

1 -9 inch pie shell, baked
2 cups sour cream
1 cup raisins
¾ cup brown sugar
1 teaspoon cinnamon
3 egg yolks
3 tablespoons flour
pinch of salt
1 teaspoon vanilla

Mix brown sugar, cinnamon, flour and salt together. Add to the sour cream, raisins, egg yolks and vanilla. Cook in a double boiler, bringing to a boil. Continue to boil until mixture is thickened. Pour into the baked pie shell.

Meringue
Whip 3 egg whites and 2 tablespoons of sugar together to form stiff peaks. Cover pie making sure meringue touches the edge of the pie crust. Bake in a 350° F. oven until lightly browned.

TROPICAL DELIGHT

3 bananas
2 eggs
1 ½ cups butter
1-19 ounce can crushed pineapple
2 cups graham wafer crumbs
2 cups icing sugar
1 teaspoon vanilla
1 large cool whip thawed
chopped walnuts, cherries and chocolate syrup

Melt ½ cup of butter and mix with wafer crumbs. Pat in 9 x 13 inch pan. Beat eggs remaining butter, icing sugar and vanilla together for about 10 minutes. Spread on wafer crust and refrigerate for 30 minutes. Soak banana slices in pineapple juice then layer on wafer crust. Next spread drained pineapple and cover with cool whip. Drizzle with chocolate syrup and sprinkle with walnuts and cherries. Refrigerate overnight.

"Live so that the preacher can tell the truth
at your funeral"   K. Bechstrom

TURTLE PECAN CHEEESECAKE

2 cups chocolate wafers, crushed

¼ cup margarine, melted

Combine and press into a 9 inch spring form pan.

Filling:

2 packages cream cheese

¾ cup sugar

1 tablespoon flour

3 eggs

2 tablespoons milk

Mix cream cheese, sugar, flour, eggs and milk in a food processor or with hand mixer. Pour over crust and bake 10 minutes at 450° F. Reduce heat to 200° F. and bake for 1 hour more.

Topping:

½ bag caramels

⅓ cup milk

Stir over low heat (or in microwave) until smooth. Cool. Pour over cooled cake.

Chocolate topping:

4 ounces Sweetened chocolate squares

1 tablespoon margarine

2 tablespoons milk

Heat over low heat or in microwave until smooth and drizzle over cake. Garnish with sliced pecans.

Cakes, Cookies and Pastries

"Birthdays are nature's way of telling us
to eat more cake."   Unknown

BANANA CHOCOLATE CHIP CAKE

1 cup butter, melted

2 cups sugar

2 eggs

4 ripe bananas, mashed

1 cup sour cream

2 teaspoons baking soda

3 cups flour

2 teaspoons baking powder

1 teaspoon vanilla

⅛ teaspoon salt

Topping: 6 ounces chocolate chips

⅓ cup brown sugar

1 teaspoon cinnamon

Mix butter, sugar, eggs, and bananas. Add baking soda to sour cream and add to mixture. Combine flour, baking powder and salt. Add flour mixture to butter mixture alternately with the sour cream mixture. Stir in vanilla. Spread half the mixture in greased and floured tube pan, then half the topping, add the rest of the batter, then the rest of the topping. Bake at 375° F. for 50-60 minutes.

BLONDE BROWNIES

1 cup sifted flour
½ teaspoon baking powder
½ teaspoon baking soda
½ teaspoon salt
1 teaspoon vanilla
½ cup nuts, chopped
⅓ cup margarine
1 cup brown sugar
1 egg, slightly beaten
1 cup chocolate chips

To sifted flour, add soda, baking powder, and salt and then sift again. Add nuts and set aside. Melt margarine and mix in sugar. Stir in eggs and vanilla. Add flour mixture gradually, mixing well. Spread batter into 9 x 9 inch greased cake pan. Sprinkle chocolate chips over the top and gently press down. Bake at 350° F. for 20 to 25 minutes. Cool in pan and cut into squares.

To change and to improve are two different things.
German Proverb

CARROT CAKE
WITH CREAM CHEESE FROSTING

2 cups brown sugar

4 eggs

2 cups flour

2 teaspoons baking powder

1 teaspoon salt

1 ½ cups canola oil

3 cups raw carrot, grated

2 teaspoons baking soda

2 teaspoons cinnamon

½ cup walnuts, chopped

Combine oil and sugar. Beat in the eggs, one at a time. Add raw carrots. Fold in sifted dry ingredients and walnuts. Bake in layer cake pans 35-40 minutes at 350° F.

Frosting:

8 ounces cream cheese

2 cups icing sugar

4 tablespoons soft butter

2 teaspoons vanilla

Soften cream cheese to room temperature and combine with butter, icing sugar and vanilla. Beat together until fluffy and spread on cooled cake.

CELEBRATION BANANA TORTE

(This is a delicious, rich banana cake with
an old-fashioned custard filling and chocolate frosting.)

1 ½ cups sugar	½ cup butter or margarine
2 eggs	¾ cup buttermilk
1 cup ripe bananas, mashed	1 teaspoon vanilla
2 cups all-purpose flour	2 teaspoons baking powder
1 teaspoon baking soda	¾ teaspoon salt

Grease and flour two round cake pans. Preheat oven to
350° F. Sift flour, baking powder, baking soda and
salt. Cream butter and gradually blend in sugar. Add
eggs, one at a time, beating after each addition. Add
mashed bananas, buttermilk and vanilla. Add flour
about one quarter at a time, alternating with banana
mixture, blending lightly after each mixture. Turn into
cake pans and bake 25-30 minutes or until inserted pick
comes out clean Let cool in pans for 5 minutes, turn
out and cool completely. Custard and icing recipes on
following page........

Custard Filling

4 egg yolks	¼ teaspoon salt
2 cups milk	3 tablespoons cornstarch
⅔ cup sugar	

Scald milk in a heavy pan or double boiler. Mix the dry ingredients with slightly beaten egg yolks. Add to the milk, stirring constantly until thick, smooth custard is formed. Cool and spread between cake layers.

Mocha Icing

2 cups icing sugar	1 teaspoon vanilla
2 tablespoons cocoa	Pinch of salt
1 teaspoon instant coffee	¼ cup butter

cream or milk to thin

Cream butter, then add the sugar alternately with flavouring and coffee. Thin with cream or milk to a spreading consistency. Mix well and spread on top and sides of cake.

"If you want anything said, ask a man. If you want anything done, ask a women." Margaret Thatcher

CHERRY ALMOND SLICE

1 ½ cups graham wafer crumbs
¾ cup margarine
½ cup sugar

Mix together and press in to 9 x 13 inch pan.

1 cup fine flaked coconut
1 can sweetened condensed sweet milk
1 cup glazed cherries, halved
1 cup slivered almonds

Sprinkle coconut on base and pour condensed milk over this. Add cherries, then a layer of slivered almonds. Bake at 350° F. for 20 minutes. Slice into squares when cooled.

"If only God would give me a clear sign! Like making a large deposit in my name at a Swiss bank." Woody Allen

CHOCOLATE CHIFFON CAKE

¾ cup boiling water mixed with ½ cup cocoa

1 ¾ cups cake flour

1 ¾ cups sugar

1 ½ teaspoons soda

1 teaspoon salt

½ cup canola oil

7 egg yolks

1 teaspoon vanilla

1 cup egg whites

½ teaspoon cream of tartar

Preheat oven to 350° F. Mix boiling water
and cocoa. Stir until smooth. Cool. Measure
and sift into mixing bowl the flour, sugar, soda
and salt. Make a well and add in order; oil, egg
yolks, cooled cocoa mixture and vanilla. Beat
until smooth, at medium speed, for 1 minute.
Beat egg whites and cream of tartar until very
stiff. Pour egg yolk mixture gradually over
beaten egg whites. Fold gently with spatula.
Pour into an ungreased tube pan. Bake 1-hour
at 350° F. When done, invert pan and cool
before removing.

COCOA FUDGE CAKE
(A good recipe for a budding chef!)

1 ⅔ cups flour

1 ½ cups white sugar

⅔ cup cocoa

1 ½ teaspoons baking soda

1 teaspoon salt

1 ½ cups buttermilk

½ cup margarine, melted

2 eggs

1 teaspoon vanilla

Measure in mixing bowl all ingredients in order listed. Blend at low speed, scrape bowl. Beat 3 minutes on high. Pour into 9 x 13 inch greased pan and bake at 350° F. for approximately 30 minutes. To test for doneness insert a wooden pick in the center of the cake; if it emerges perfectly clean, the cake is done. Ice with caramel icing on next page.

CARAMEL ICING

⅓ cup butter

1 cup brown sugar

⅓ cup cream

1 ½ cups icing sugar

In saucepan bring butter, brown sugar and cream
to a boil and continue to simmer for 2 minutes.
Remove from heat and beat in the icing sugar.
Spread on cooled cake.

TOP TEN THINGS ONLY WOMEN UNDERSTAND
10. Cats' facial expressions.
9. The need for the same style of shoes in
different colors.
8. Why bean sprouts aren't just weeds.
7. Fat clothes.
6. Taking a car trip without trying to beat your
best time.
5. The difference between beige, ecru, cream,
off-white, and eggshell.
4. Cutting your hair to make it grow.
3. Eyelash curlers.
2. The inaccuracy of every bathroom scale ever
made.
AND, the Number One Number One thing only
women understand:
1. OTHER WOMEN

CREAM FILLED MERINGUE CAKE

(This is a very sweet, rich, yummy dessert that is nothing to prepare- especially if you do the meringues a few days ahead.)

4 large egg whites, at room temperature

1 teaspoon vanilla

¼ teaspoon cream of tartar

¼ teaspoon salt

1 cup sugar

½ cup chocolate syrup-prepared sundae topping works well

2 cups whipping cream, whipped

2 cups fruit -strawberries and kiwi are great.

Line 2 baking sheets with foil. Draw 3 nine-inch circles on the foil. In a large glass or metal bowl, beat egg whites, vanilla, cream of tartar and salt at high speed until soft peaks form. Gradually beat in sugar, beating well after each addition and continue beating until stiff, glossy peaks form. Divide the meringue into 3 dollops onto prepared cookie sheets within your marked circles. Smooth out until it looks like 3 large cookies. Bake in preheated Continued on next page..........

CREAM FILLED MERINGUE CAKE

continued.......

oven at 250° F for 1¼ to 1½ hours until
crisp and firm to the touch. Turn off heat
and allow to cool with door propped open.
  Meringues can be made ahead and at this
point stored in an airtight container for several
days at room temperature. When you are
ready to assemble the cake (approximately 2
hours before serving) spread chocolate syrup
over the bottom 2 of the meringues. Put the
plain meringue on a serving plate and cover
with a layer of whipped cream and a layer of
fruit. Add a chocolate-painted meringue and
repeat. Add last meringue and cover with
whipped cream. Hint - The only trick to this
dessert is to try to stick to the 2 hour ahead
preparation time. If you prepare too much
earlier than that, the meringues get too soft,
and too much later, they are too crispy.

One day my "housework-challenged" husband decided to
wash his sweatshirt. Seconds after he stepped into the
laundry room, he shouted to me, "What setting do I use on
the washing machine?"
"It depends," I replied. "What does it say on your shirt?"
He yelled back, "University of Regina"
(Yikes! -where do you start)

DEVIL'S FOOD CAKE
WITH MOCHA ICING

3 cups sifted cake flour

½ teaspoon salt

1 cup margarine or butter

2 cups brown sugar, packed

2 eggs

¼ cup cocoa

2 teaspoons vanilla

2 cups buttermilk

2 teaspoons baking soda

Cream butter, sugar, eggs, cocoa and vanilla.
Dissolve soda in buttermilk and add to butter
mixture. Add sifted flour and salt. Beat well.
Divide batter between 2 greased and floured 8
inch layer pans. Bake at 350° F. for about
30 minutes or until an inserted toothpick comes
out clean. Cool. Layer cake or cut into 4
layers and fill with Mocha Icing.

Continued on next page..............

MOCHA ICING

½ cup chocolate chips
2 tablespoons hot water
2 teaspoons instant coffee
¼ cup sugar
large container Cool Whip

Melt chocolate chips with hot water, add coffee
and sugar. Stir until smooth. When cool, fold in
large container Cool Whip. Spread icing
between the layers and on top...it is not
necessary to ice the sides as the layers look
attractive. Decorate with grated chocolate.

*When women are the adviser, the lords of creation
don't take on the advice till they have persuaded
themselves that it is just what they intended to do;
then they act upon it, and if it succeeds, they give
the weaker vessel half the credit of it; if it fails,
they generously give her the whole"*
Louisa May Alcott

FIFTIETH BIRTHDAY CAKE

(or 20, 30 or 40 – this is one everybody loves-but at age 50 you have a little more time so you don't have to use a mix)

½ cup poppy seed

1 cup milk

¾ cup butter or margarine

1 ½ cups sugar

2 cups flour

2 teaspoons baking powder

4 egg whites, beaten stiff

1 teaspoon almond flavoring or vanilla

Put the poppy seeds in the milk and let soak for at least one hour. Cream butter and add sugar, then add milk and poppy seeds. Add dry ingredients. Beat until blended, then fold in beaten egg whites.   Bake in two round layer cake pans at 375° F. for 20-30 minutes or until a toothpick comes out clean when inserted into the middle. Fill with a custard filling....next page and ice with buttercream icing.

Why does it take one million sperm to fertilize one egg?   -Because sperm are male and they refuse to ask directions.

Shown on previous page:

- Citrus Slush... page 24
- Ice Ring for Punches... page 28
- Coconut Cheese Ball...page 5

CUSTARD FILLING

4 egg yolks   ¼ teaspoon salt
2 cups milk   3 tablespoons cornstarch
⅔ cup sugar

Scald milk in a heavy pan or double boiler. Mix the dry
ingredients with slightly beaten egg yolks. Add to the
milk, stirring constantly until thick and a smooth custard
is formed. Cool and spread between cake layers.

BUTTERCREAM FROSTING

1 - 16 ounce package icing sugar
6 tablespoons butter or margarine, softened
3 to 4 tablespoons cream or milk
1 ½ teaspoons vanilla extract
⅛ teaspoon salt

At medium speed in a large bowl, beat all ingredients
until smooth, adding more milk or cream if necessary to
make a good consistency to spread.
* You can flavour this icing by substituting lemon or
orange juice and omitting vanilla and milk.

FOUR GENERATION'S LIGHT CHRISTMAS CAKE

3 pounds light sultana raisins

2½ pounds red and green cherries

1½ pounds glazed fruit

2 packages gumdrops

1 pound blanched almonds

2½ cups fine coconut

1½ cups butter

3 cups white sugar

9 eggs

1 large can crushed pineapple

4 teaspoons vanilla

4½ cups flour

1 teaspoon baking powder

Measure first 6 ingredients into large bowl. Sprinkle ½ cup of the flour over fruit. Stir to coat the fruit with flour. Cream butter and sugar in large mixing bowl. Beat in eggs 1 at a time. Add remaining ingredients in order given. Add fruit mixture being gentle so you don't crush the cherries. Line 4 loaf pans with foil, grease and fill about ¾ full. Bake at 250°F. for 4 hours or until a wooden pick comes out clean. (Place a tin can of water in the oven to keep the cakes from drying out while baking.)

KUCHAN
(A traditional German cake.)

3 cups all-purpose flour

2 teaspoons baking powder

½ teaspoon salt

1 cup shortening

2 eggs

1 cup milk

1 teaspoon vanilla

10 – 12 apples, peeled and sliced

Sugar and cinnamon to taste

Mix flour, baking powder, salt and shortening as for pie crust. Add eggs, milk and vanilla. Roll ½-inch thick and spread on two cookie sheets. Cover with 1 or 2 layers of peeled sliced apples. Add sugar and cinnamon.

Topping: 1 cup butter

2 cups sugar

2 cups flour

Mix well with hands and spread crumbs over apples. Bake at 375° F. 25 minutes or until brown. Cool. Remove from pan. (You can substitute fresh peaches for the apples.)

LEMON CHIFFON CAKE

Cake:

1 ½ cups all-purpose flour
1 tablespoon baking powder
1 teaspoon salt
½ cup sugar
½ cup oil
6 eggs yolks
¾ cup water
1 tablespoon grated lemon rind
6 egg whites
½ teaspoon cream of tartar
¾ cup sugar

Filling:

1 cup whipping cream
2 ½ cups Lemon pie filling
prepared lemon slices to garnish

Cake:

Combine flour, baking powder, salt and ½ cup sugar in large mixer bowl. Stir well to blend. Add oil, egg yolks, water and lemon rind. Beat with electric mixer until smooth (about 30 seconds). Beat in small mixing

Continued on next page..............

Lemon Chiffon Cake continued..........

bowl, egg whites and cream of tartar to form stiff but moist peaks. Gradually add ¾ cup sugar, beating until very stiff and shiny peaks are formed. Fold egg whites into egg yolk mixture gently but thoroughly. Turn batter into ungreased 10" tube pan. Bake at 350°F. for 60 minutes, or until toothpick inserted in center comes out clean. Invert and cool cake completely in pan. When cool, loosen edges and shake pan to remove cake.

Filling:
Beat cream to stiff peaks. Fold in lemon filling. Chill if necessary until stiff.

Assembly:
Slice cake horizontally into 3 equal layers. Fill layers with ⅓ of filling. Spread remaining filling on top layer. Decorate top with lemon slices.

"Age does not protect you from love; but love, to some extent, protects you from age." Moreau

MAPLE WALNUT ZUCHINNI CAKE

1 cup brown sugar

1 cup white sugar

1 cup canola oil

3 eggs

1 teaspoon vanilla

2-3 teaspoons maple flavoring

2 cups zucchini, peeled and shredded

3 cups flour

1 teaspoon baking soda

¼ teaspoon baking powder

½ teaspoon salt

1 cup walnuts, chopped

Mix together sugars and oil. Beat in eggs one at a time. Add vanilla and maple flavoring. Stir in zucchini. Stir in flour, baking soda, baking powder and salt until well blended. Add walnuts. Bake in a greased cookie sheet at 350° F for 20-30 minutes. Ice with Cream Cheese Icing using 1 ½ teaspoons maple flavoring.

MOLASSES LAYER CAKE

(Although this cake recipe requires some time for
preparation and assembly, it is well worth it.)

½ cup butter

1 cup brown sugar

2 tablespoons molasses

2 cups flour

2 teaspoons baking soda

¾ cup buttermilk

3 egg whites, beaten until stiff

Cream butter, sugar and molasses. Stir together
the flour and baking soda. Add to butter mixture
alternately with the buttermilk. Fold into the
beaten egg whites. Pour into 2 greased layer
cake pans and bake in a 350° F. oven for 25-
30 minutes.

Filling: ¾ cup raisins   3 egg yolks
        1 teaspoon vanilla   ¾ cup milk
        1 tablespoon butter

Boil together until thick and spread between cake
layers.

Icing: 1 cup butter
       3 tablespoons brown sugar
       3 tablespoons cream

Bring to a boil and simmer for 10 minutes.
Beat well. Pour over cake.

NUSIN BUTTER
(Traditional German Apple Cake)

¾ cup shortening
1 teaspoon baking powder
2 eggs, separated
2 cups flour
¼ cup cream
1 cup raisins
3 large apples, peeled, cored and sliced
½ cup sugar
Sprinkle of cinnamon and sugar.

Sift dry ingredients, mix in shortening as for pie dough. Beat egg yolks with a little cream and work in, to make a workable dough. Divide in half. Roll out thin to fit a 11 x 9 inch pan. Cook raisins apples and sugar together for a few minutes. Put on dough. Top with other half of thinly rolled dough. Beat egg whites until foamy and brush on the top of the cake. Sprinkle with sugar and cinnamon. Bake at 350° F for about 25 minutes.

ORANGE CAKE

(This is a rich, delicious cake. It is showy when
decorated with creamy frosting and orange slices.)

1 ¾ cups pre-sifted flour

2 ½ teaspoons baking powder

½ teaspoon salt

½ cup margarine or butter

2 tablespoons grated orange zest

1 cup sugar

½ teaspoon vanilla

2 eggs

½ cup milk

½ cup orange juice

Preheat oven to 350°. Measure flour, baking powder
and salt. Set aside. In mixing bowl cream margarine,
and add sugar gradually, mixing until creamy. Add
orange zest and vanilla. Add eggs, beating well after
each. Add dry ingredients and egg mixture alternately
with milk and juice. Beat well after each. Spread evenly
in 2 greased round layer pans. Bake for 25-30
minutes until toothpick comes out clean.

*This is also delicious filled with a chocolate ganache.
Recipes for fillings and frosting continued on next
page...

CREAMY WHITE FROSTING

2 tablespoons water
4 ½ tablespoons sugar
Heat until sugar is dissolved
Mix in bowl:
2 ½ cups icing sugar
⅔ cup margarine, softened
1 egg
1 teaspoon vanilla
Mix well, gradually add sugar and water. Beat again.
Keeps in fridge for up to two weeks.

CHOCOLATE GANACHE
(Ganache is a fancy term for rich chocolate icing made
of semisweet chocolate and whipping cream.)

⅓ cups butter
⅔ cups heavy cream
12 ounces sweetened chocolate, chopped
Melt butter with cream. When completely melted, take
off the heat and stir in chocolate until melted and pour
about ⅓ mixture between the layers of cake and the
remainder over the assembled cake. YUM!

PINEAPPLE CARROT CAKE
(A great recipe for wedding cakes.)

4 eggs

2 cups sugar

1 ¼ cups canola oil

1 teaspoon vanilla

1 ½ cups carrots, grated

1 cup crushed pineapple, drained

2 cups flour

1 teaspoon baking soda

1 teaspoon cinnamon

½ teaspoon nutmeg

¼ teaspoon allspice

¼ teaspoon cloves

¼ teaspoon salt

Beat together eggs, sugar, oil and vanilla. Add carrots and pineapple and mix. Sift together; flour, soda, cinnamon, nutmeg, allspice, cloves and salt. Add to egg mixture and stir till smooth. Bake in a greased 9x13-inch pan at 350°F. oven for about 1 hour. Delicious with cream cheese icing.

PRIZE ANGEL FOOD CAKE

(A special lady shared this and is still famous for this cake at age 86.)

Sift together (twice):

1 cup and 2 tablespoons sifted cake flour

¾ cup sugar

Put into a large bowl:

11-13 egg whites, depending on the size of the egg

½ teaspoon salt

Beat on high speed until foamy (½ minute) and add 1½ teaspoons cream of tartar. Continue beating until whites are stiff and stand in points (about 2½ to 3 minutes).

Sprinkle in quickly:

1 cup sifted sugar — beat until blended (about 1 minute).

Turn to lowest speed and add:

1 teaspoon vanilla

1 teaspoon almond extract

Sprinkle in sifted dry ingredients evenly and quickly. Beat only enough to blend about 1 ½ minutes. Put into 10 inch tube pan. Release air bubbles by cutting through cake batter with a knife.

Bake at 375° F. for 30 to 35 minutes.

Remove from oven and invert upside down until cake is completely cooled.

PONNUKOKUR

(This traditional Icelandic treat is generally
served as a dainty with coffee.)

2 eggs
½ cup white sugar
¼ teaspoon salt
½ teaspoon cinnamon
½ teaspoon baking soda
1 teaspoon baking powder
½ teaspoon vanilla
½ cup sour cream
1½ cups flour
2 cups milk

Beat eggs, sugar, salt, baking powder, vanilla and
cinnamon in a bowl (or a food processor works
excellent). Dissolve soda in a bit of boiling water and
mix in sour cream. Add the flour gradually, alternating
and ending with the milk. This makes a very thin
batter. Pour ½ cup of batter into a well-greased hot
non-stick frying pan. Spread the batter to make a very
thin crepe. Flip the cake when slightly browned.
Sprinkle with a white sugar and cinnamon mixture and
roll. Makes about 2 dozen crepes.

POPPY SEED BUNDT
(This starts with a mix — but you would never know it by the end product.)

Deluxe white cake mix
1 cup canola oil
1 package lemon instant pudding
4 eggs
½ cup poppy seed
½ cup water

Grease and flour a bundt cake pan.
Beat all ingredients together, and pour into bundt pan. Bake for 1 hour at 350° F.
Drizzle lemon glaze over the cake while still warm.

Lemon Glaze
1 ½ cups icing sugar
4 to 5 teaspoons fresh lemon juice
1 ½ teaspoons fresh lemon zest, grated

FROSTED BROWNIES

1 cup butter, melted
2 cups brown sugar
4 tablespoons cocoa
2 eggs
1 cup flour

Mix all together. Bake in a greased 9 x 11 inch pan at 350° F. for 20 – 25 min. Ice with icing while still hot.

Icing:
2 tablespoons butter
1 – 1 ½ cups icing sugar
3 tablespoons cocoa
3 tablespoons boiling water
1 teaspoon vanilla
Mix together. Pour over brownies while still hot.

PUMPKIN CAKE
WITH CREAM CHEESE ICING

4 eggs
2 cups white sugar
1 cup canola oil
1 – 14 ounce can pumpkin
2 cups flour
2 teaspoons baking soda
½ teaspoon salt
½ teaspoon cloves
2 teaspoons cinnamon
½ teaspoon ginger
½ teaspoon nutmeg

Beat eggs until frothy and add sugar. Beat for 1 minute and add oil and pumpkin slowly, beating well. Add remaining ingredients; stir until moistened. Turn into a greased and floured 10 inch angel food tube pan. Bake at 350° F. for about 1 hour or until inserted wooden toothpick comes out clean. Let stand 20 minutes and remove from pan to cool. Ice with Cream Cheese Icing.

Continued on next page...........

CREAM CHEESE ICING

1 – 8 ounce package cream cheese, softened
4 cups icing sugar
¼ cup margarine, softened
1 teaspoon vanilla

Put all ingredients in mixing bowl. Beat slowly at first and then at medium speed until light and fluffy. More or less icing sugar may be added as desired.

"I understand more and more how true Daddy's words were when he said "All children must look after their own upbringing. Parents can only give good advice or put them on the right paths."
Anne Frank

RIBBON SQUARES

(There are lots of these recipes with slight
variations- this is the best!)

Bottom layer:

½ cup butter

¼ cup sugar

5 tablespoons cocoa

1 egg, beaten

1 teaspoon vanilla

1 ¾ - 2 cups graham wafer crumbs

½ cup walnuts, chopped

Cook butter, sugar, cocoa, vanilla and egg in
saucepan over low heat. Stir constantly, until
mixture begins to thicken. Remove from heat and
add graham crumbs and nuts. Pat firmly into a
9 x 9 inch pan. Chill for at least 1 hour.

Middle Layer:

½ cup butter, creamed

2 tablespoons vanilla instant pudding mix

3 tablespoons milk

2 cups icing sugar

Cream butter, pudding and milk.

Continued on next page...........

Gradually add icing sugar to make a smooth spreading consistency. Spread over first layer in pan. Chill until firm.

Topping:
4 squares semi-sweet chocolate
2 tablespoons butter.

Melt chocolate and butter together, stirring until smooth. Drizzle chocolate over filling. Chill. Makes about 30 bars.

"You must not lose faith in humanity. Humanity is an ocean; if a few drops of the ocean are dirty, the ocean does not become dirty." Mahatma Ghandi

RHUBARB CAKE
(A first taste of spring)

1 ½ cups brown sugar
1 cup butter or margarine, softened
2 eggs
1 teaspoon vanilla
½ cup milk, scalded and cooled
2 cups flour
1 teaspoon baking soda
¼ teaspoon salt
2 generous cups rhubarb, chopped
½ cup sugar
1 tablespoon cinnamon

Beat together butter and sugar. Add eggs and vanilla. Mix in milk. Stir in dry ingredients; fold in rhubarb. Pour into a greased and floured 9x13-inch cake pan. Top with the ½ cup sugar and cinnamon. Bake in a 325°F. oven for 30-35 minutes.

RHUBARB FILLED CAKE

Base: 2 cups flour

½ cup butter

¼ teaspoon salt

1 teaspoon baking powder

1 egg, beaten

Filling: 1 cup sugar

½ cup flour

2 eggs beaten

5 cups washed, chopped rhubarb

¼ cup butter, melted

¼ cup cream-milk or canned milk

Mix base with fork, save 1 cup for top of cake.
Flatten the rest into a 9 x 13 inch greased pan.
Mix filling ingredients in order given.
Pour over mixture in pan.
Cover with reserved 1 cup topping.
Sprinkle top with cinnamon and sugar.
Bake at 325° F. for 45 minutes.

DECADENT CARAMEL
SHORTBREAD SQUARE

(This is a rich, absolutely heavenly treat-but you can smell the calories as it bakes!)

Base:

½ pound butter

⅔ cup sugar

2 cups flour

Mix together until crumbly. Pat in buttered 9 x 13 inch buttered pan. Preheat oven to 350°F. and bake for 15 minutes or until golden, watch closely.

Second Layer:

½ pound butter

⅔ cup sugar

4 tablespoons corn syrup

1 tin sweetened condensed milk

Combine all ingredients in a saucepan over medium heat and bring to a slow boil for 5 minutes stirring constantly. Remove from heat and beat until smooth approximately 5 minutes. Pour over base and cool.

Top Layer:

12 ounces semi sweet chocolate chips

2 tablespoons butter

Melt slowly in saucepan and spread on caramel layer.

Hint- Use real butter, do not substitute margarine.

SASKATOON PRAIRIE BERRYCAKE

Filling: 4 cups fresh or frozen saskatoons

    ¾ cup sugar

    1 tablespoon lemon juice

    ½ teaspoon cinnamon

    3 tablespoons cornstarch, with ¼ cup water

In a saucepan cook saskatoons over moderate heat for 10 minutes. Add sugar, lemon juice and cinnamon. Cook for 2 more minutes. Add cornstarch mixture. Stir until thickened. Cool.

Batter: 1 cup butter

    1 ¾ cups white sugar

    4 eggs

    1 teaspoon vanilla

    1 teaspoon almond extract

    3 cups flour

Beat butter and sugar. Add eggs 1 at a time. Add vanilla and almond extract. Add flour, 1 cup at a time. until batter is quite stiff. Spread ⅔ of batter on a buttered cookie sheet. Carefully spread cooled saskatoon filling on batter. Drop spoonfuls on remaining batter here and there on top, spread a bit, but leave openings. Bake at 350°F. for 40 minutes or until golden brown.

VINATARTE
(A traditional Icelandic cake.)

1 cup butter

1 ½ cups sugar

2 eggs

4 cups flour

1 teaspoon baking powder

¼ teaspoon ground cardamom

1 teaspoon vanilla

3 tablespoons whipping cream

Cream butter, add sugar, then eggs one at a time beating after each. Sift flour with baking powder and cardamom. Add a little of the sifted flour mixture to the butter mixture, beating after adding. Add vanilla and cream, then work in the remaining flour. Divide dough into 6 equal parts and roll on lightly floured surface or pat into 9 inch greased layer pan. Bake at 375°F. until delicate brown. Put together with prune filling, below. Allow to mellow for a few days. You can ice cake if you wish.

Prune Filling:

1 pound pitted prunes

½ cup sugar

Continued on next page.............

VINATARTE continued...........

1 tablespoon cinnamon

½ cup prune juice

1 tablespoon vanilla

Cook prunes in water. When softened, remove from heat and puree in blender. Add sugar, cinnamon and ½ cup of juice in which the prunes were cooked. Return all ingredients to pot and cook together, add vanilla and cool. Spread between cooked layers of cake.

PEANUT CLUSTERS
(Crunchy and oh soooo chocolatey!!!!!)

6 ounces semi-sweet chocolate

6 ounces caramel chips

4 ounce Chinese noodles, dry

8 ounces salted peanuts, skinless

Melt chocolate and caramel chips in a double boiler, add noodles and nuts. Remove from heat, but keep over the hot water.. Drop by teaspoon on wax paper and cool.

SCRUMPTIOUS MARBLE SQUARES

½ cup margarine

¾ cup water

3 tablespoons cocoa...bring to a boil over medium heat.

2 ¼ cups flour

1 ½ cups sugar

1 teaspoon soda

½ teaspoon salt

Sift together and add to above mixture....mix well.

2 eggs, beaten

½ cup sour cream

Add to above and mix well

Pour into greased and floured 15 x 10 inch cookie sheet.

Topping: 1 – 8 ounce cream cheese

⅓ cup sugar

1 egg

Cream together and drizzle over cake. Cut through with knife to get marbled effect, making sure cheese mixture gets right to edge. Sprinkle with grated chocolate or chocolate chips. Bake at 350° F. for 25 minutes or until done.

DUTCH COOKIES

1 cup butter

1 cup sugar

1 egg

pinch of salt

2 teaspoons cinnamon

1 teaspoon vanilla

2 cups flour

Cream butter and sugar. Add remaining ingredients.
Roll into small balls as this is a sweet rich cookie. Place
on a greased cookie sheet. Flatten cookies with floured
fork to give waffle appearance (the flatter, the better).
Bake at 350 °F. for 8 – 12 minutes.

Filling:

½ cup butter

½ cup brown sugar

1 teaspoon cinnamon

¼ cup corn syrup

Mix in saucepan. Heat until brown sugar is dissolved.
Cool, then spread between cookies.

FAVORITE SUGAR COOKIES

2 cups sugar
1 pound butter
4 eggs
5 cups flour
2 teaspoons baking soda
1 teaspoon salt
4 teaspoons cream of tartar
¼ teaspoon nutmeg

Cream sugar and butter. Add eggs one at a time, beating after each egg. Sift together the flour, baking soda, salt, cream of tartar and nutmeg. Add to butter mixture. Knead to make a soft dough. Chill. Roll out on lightly floured surface to ¼ inch thickness. Cut into shapes with floured cookie cutter. Bake at 375° F. for 6-8 minutes. Decorate as desired. (If you don't want to ice the cookie, sprinkle with coarse sugar before baking.)

GINGERSNAPS

1 cup white sugar

¾ cup margarine, softened

1 egg

4 tablespoons molasses

2 cups flour

1 teaspoon salt

2 teaspoons baking soda

1 teaspoon cinnamon

1 teaspoon cloves

1 teaspoon ginger

Cream together the sugar, margarine, eggs and molasses until fluffy. Sift together dry ingredients and add to creamed mixture. Roll small (walnut-sized) balls of dough in sugar and bake on a greased cookie sheet in 350°F oven for approximately 12 minutes.

"Committee – a group who can individually do nothing, but as a group can decide nothing can be done."   *Fred Allen*

HEALTHY CHOCOLATE CHIP COOKIES

2 cup whole wheat flour

1 teaspoon soda

2 cups oatmeal

¼ cup wheat germ

¾ cup margarine

1 ½ cups brown sugar

2 eggs

1 cup chocolate chips

½ cup flax

Optional:

½ cup chopped nuts

½ cup raisins

Cream margarine, brown sugar, and eggs. Add rest of dry ingredients. Drop by spoonfuls on greased cookie sheet. Flatten with a fork. Bake at 350°F for 12 to 15 minutes. Makes approximately 3 dozen.

JAM - JAM COOKIES

1 cup brown sugar
1 cup butter
2 eggs
½ cup corn syrup
2 teaspoons baking soda
1 teaspoon lemon extract
3-4 cups flour

Cream butter, sugar, eggs, syrup and lemon extract. Add baking soda, and enough flour to make a soft dough. Roll out and cut with a round cookie cutter. Bake at 350° F. for 10-12 minutes. While warm, sandwich cookies with your favorite jam.

"When you play, play hard; when you work, don't play at all."   Theodore Roosevelt

JUMBO RAISIN COOKIES

1 cup water
2 cups raisins
1 cup shortening
2 cups white sugar
3 eggs
1 teaspoon vanilla
4 cups flour
1 teaspoon baking powder
1 teaspoon baking soda
2 teaspoons salt
1 ½ teaspoons cinnamon
¼ teaspoon nutmeg
¼ teaspoon allspice
1 cup nuts (optional)

Combine water and raisins and boil for 5 minutes. Let cool. In large mixing bowl, combine sugar, shortening, eggs and vanilla. Beat at medium speed until well blended. Add raisins, flour, baking soda, baking powder, spices and salt. Beat at low speed until soft dough forms. Drop dough by heaping teaspoons 2 inches apart onto prepared cookie sheets. Bake at 400° F. for 10-12 minutes, or until light brown.

LOWER FAT CHOCOLATE CHIP
SCRUMPTIOUS COOKIES

½ cup margarine

½ cup plain yogurt

⅔ cup brown sugar

2 eggs

1½ cups flour

1 teaspoon salt

1 teaspoon baking soda

1 cup chocolate chips

1 teaspoon vanilla

⅓ cup chopped nuts

2 cups oatmeal.

Cream margarine and yogurt. Add sugar.
Gradually add eggs, beat well. Add vanilla.
Sift flour salt and soda. Add dry ingredients to creamed
mixture. Add nuts, chocolate chips and oatmeal.
Drop by teaspoonfuls on cookie sheet which has been
sprayed with oil spray. Bake at 350° F. for 10-12
minutes.

LUSCIOUS LEMON COOKIES

3 cups flour
3 tablespoons cornstarch
3/4 teaspoon salt
1½ cups butter
1 cup icing sugar
1 tablespoon lemon zest, grated
1½ teaspoons lemon extract
1/4 teaspoon almond extract

Preheat oven to 325° F. Combine flour, cornstarch, and salt, and set aside. In large bowl, beat butter and sugar until creamy, occasionally scraping bowl with rubber spatula. Beat in lemon zest and extracts. Reduce speed to low; gradually beat in the flour mixture until blended, occasionally scraping bowl.
Divide dough in half. Between two sheets of waxed paper, roll half of the dough ⅜ inch thick. (If paper wrinkles during rolling, peel it off, then replace it to remove wrinkles.)
With floured cookie cutter, cut dough into cookies. With lightly floured wide spatula, carefully place cookies 1 inch apart, on ungreased large cookie sheet.
Continued on next page..............

LUSCIOUS LEMON COOKIES continued....

(If dough becomes too soft to transfer to cookie sheet, freeze 10 minutes until it's firm.) Bake cookies approximately 15 minutes or until edges are golden. Transfer cookies to a wire rack; cool 10 minutes.

Lemon Glaze

1 ½ cups icing sugar
4 to 5 teaspoons fresh lemon juice
1 ½ teaspoons lemon zest

In a small bowl, mix icing sugar, lemon juice, and lemon zest until blended. Drizzle glaze over cookies. Allow glaze to set about 20 minutes.

"The greater obstacle to discovery is not ignorance — it is the illusion of knowledge." Daniel J. Boorstin

FAVORITE CHRISTMAS SHORTBREAD
(This is a very simple recipe for a whipped shortbread — but tested against some more complicated recipes-this one came out the winner.)

1 pound butter (not margarine)
½ cup corn starch
3 cups flour
1 cup sifted icing sugar

Soften and cream butter, slowly add dry ingredients. Beat until smooth. Drop by teaspoon onto cookie sheet and flatten with fork dipped in flour. Bake in preheated oven 350° F. for 12 minutes or until just before they begin to brown. (You may see a little golden around the edges but these cookies should still be white.) May be decorated with sprinkles or half a maraschino cherry prior to baking.
*Try something new. Form this dough into logs about 6 inches longs and two inches in diameter. (work with the dough as little as possible) Then roll the log in colored sugar — some red and some green and slice them into coins about ½ inch thick. Bake at 350°F for 10-12 minutes. They look so nice on a serving plate.

CELEBRATION BUTTER TARTS

2 eggs
2 cups brown sugar
2 tablespoons vinegar
1 teaspoon vanilla
½ cup butter, melted
1 ½ cups raisins
(½ cup walnuts can be substituted for ½ cup of
the raisins.)

Beat eggs well. Add sugar, vinegar and vanilla.
Stir in melted butter and raisins. Fill unbaked
tart shells ½-full. Bake at 450°F. for 8-10
minutes, reduce heat to 350°F. and bake for
another 15-20 minutes until filling is firm.

*"Make the best use of what is in your power, and
take the rest as it happens."*   *Epictetus*

DANISH PUFF

Bottom layer:
1 cup sifted flour
½ cup butter or margarine
2 tablespoons water
Cut butter into flour. Sprinkle water over mixture. Mix well with fork. Form into ball. Divide in half. On an ungreased baking sheet pat each half into a strip 12x3 inches. Strips should be about 3 inches apart.

Top layer:
½ cup butter or margarine
1 cup water
1 teaspoon almond flavoring
1 cup flour
3 eggs
In medium saucepan bring butter and water to a rolling boil. Remove from heat and quickly stir in almond flavoring and flour. Stir vigorously over low heat until the mixture forms a ball, about 1 minute. Remove from heat and beat in eggs, one at a time, until smooth. Divide in half; spread
(Continued on next page...............)

each half evenly over the strips, covering completely. Bake in a 350° F. oven about 60 minutes or until topping is crisp and brown.

Glaze:

1 ½ cups icing sugar

2 tablespoons butter, softened

1 ½ teaspoons almond flavoring

1 to 2 tablespoons warm water

Sliced almonds

Combine icing sugar with butter. Add almond flavoring. Beat, gradually adding 1 to 2 tablespoons of water, until smooth. When the strips have cooled, frost them with the glaze and sprinkle generously with almonds. Serves 12.

"Mature people are made not out of good times but out of bad times."   *H. J. Schachtel*

SHORTBREAD LEMON TARTS

1 cup butter
½ cup icing sugar
1 ½ cups flour
1 tablespoon cornstarch

Mix ingredients in blender for a few seconds until pastry forms a ball. Do not roll. Pat into tiny muffin tins (1 ½-inches in diameter) with your finger to form shell. Prick bottoms with fork and bake in 325°F. oven for 20 minutes. If shells puff up during baking prick again and return to oven. These freeze well.

Lemon Filling:
2 eggs, well beaten
½ cup butter
1 cup sugar
Juice of 2 lemons and a bit of peel
Combine all ingredients in pot and bring to a boil. Reduce heat to low and cook for 15 minutes, stirring constantly. Cover and cool in fridge. Fill shells as needed. This filling will keep well in the fridge for up to two weeks.

FAILPROOF PIE CRUST

2 cups shortening or lard
5 cups flour
1 teaspoon salt
1 tablespoon brown sugar
1 egg
1 tablespoon vinegar

Rub shortening and flour together. Beat egg and add vinegar, pour into a measuring cup and add enough water to mixture to make ¾ cup. Gradually add liquid to flour mixture until it forms a dough. Work as little as possible. Dough may be stored in refrigerator or in freezer. Chill and roll out on floured surface. Prick crust all over with a fork if baking empty. Bake at 400° F. for 10 to 15 minutes. Yields: 6 pie shells or 3 to 4 double crust pies.

I have often regretted my speech, but never my silence. Publius Syrus

The good news on the breast cancer front:

- Mortality rates from breast cancer are currently at their lowest since 1950.
- The average five-year survival rate for women with breast cancer is 82%.
- Since 1986, mortality rates have declined by an estimated 23%.
- Incidence rates have begun to stabilize over the last ten years, but do continue to increase.
- We now know that lifestyle choices, such as not smoking, healthy eating and staying physically active, can play an important role in reducing breast cancer risk.

Reproduced with the permission of the Canadian Breast Cancer Foundation, National Office, 2004.

Treats

"Hugs can do great amounts of good —
especially for children."
Princess Dianna

This chapter is a selection of recipes that the kids or grandkids ask for when they are coming home for holidays. Not necessarily nutritious but when served with other good food as a treat, make coming home to Moms or Grandmas a little more special.

AWESOME BUTTERSCOTCH SAUCE
(On ice cream sundaes or as a fresh fruit dip, this sauce is truly awesome.)

Combine:
1 cup brown sugar
1 cup golden corn syrup
½ cup cream
2 tablespoons butter

The key to this sauce is to bring it to a gentle boil for 5 minutes. Remove from heat and add vanilla.
You will have 2 – 2 ½ cups of superb sauce.

BIRTHDAY WORM CAKE

1 package of cream filled cookies
¼ cup butter or hard margarine at room temperature
8 ounce package cream cheese, softened
1 cup icing sugar
1 teaspoon vanilla
4 packages chocolate instant pudding (4 serving)
6 cups milk
4 ⅓ cups frozen whipped topping, thawed
Gummy worms

Put the cookies in a food processor or blender. Process until they become fine crumbs. Set aside. Put the butter, cream cheese, icing sugar and vanilla in a bowl. Beat on low speed to mix, then beat on medium speed until smooth. Add the chocolate pudding powders and the milk. Beat on low to combine. Fold the whipped topping into the pudding mixture with a spatula. In a large bowl, assemble in layers as follows:
1. ⅓ cookie crumbs   2. ½ pudding mixture
3. ⅓ cookie crumbs   4. ½ pudding mixture
5. ⅓ cookie crumbs Place gummy worms on top. Chill at least 3 hours before serving.

Shown on previous page:

- Gumdrop Popcorn Cake...page 359
- Special Cone Cakes... page 353
- Secret Milk Recipe... page 354

Cookie Plate

- Jumbo Raisin Cookies... page 336
- Peanut Clusters... page 329
- Jam Jams.... Page 335
- Scuffles...page 70
- Ginger Snaps... page 333
- Favorite Christmas Shortbread... page 340

CHOCOLATE SANDWICH COOKIES
(The kids' first choice!)

2 boxes Devils Food cake mix
4 eggs, beaten
1 cup canola oil

Mix well and roll into balls about nickel size.
(They will be oily.) Bake balls at 350° F. for 10 to
12 minutes. Let cool on pan, then remove.
Ice together with cream cheese filling.

CREAM CHEESE FILLING

1 - 8 ounce package cream cheese, softened
3 - 4 cups icing sugar
3 tablespoons margarine
1 teaspoon vanilla

Mix together until creamy smooth. Spread liberally
on cooled cookie bottom and sandwich with
another cookie.

COFFEE CRISP SQUARES

1 tablespoon peanut butter
½ package chocolate chips
½ package butterscotch chips
4 cups Rice Krispies
Melt chips and peanut butter and add Rice Krispies.
Pack into an 8 x 8 inch pan and let harden. This cuts
nicely for lunches or picnics.

CREAMY POPCORN BALLS
(Delicious!!)

4 tablespoons butter
1 cup brown sugar
½ cup light corn syrup
⅔ cup sweetened condensed milk
½ teaspoon vanilla
20 cups popped corn

Combine butter, sugar and syrup. Stir to boiling over
medium heat. Stir in sweetened milk, simmer; stir
constantly until soft-ball stage when dropped in cold
water. (234° F. – 238° F.) Stir in vanilla. Pour
over popped corn and mix well. Butter hands and shape
into balls. Makes approximately 15 balls. Enjoy.

BREAKFAST BARS

5 cups corn flakes
1 cup sliced almonds
1 cup coconut
(Other cereals and nuts may be substituted)

Place in large bowl.

1 small package of mini-marshmallows
½ cup margarine or butter, melted
1 teaspoon vanilla

Melt marshmallows in butter or margarine. Add vanilla
and dry ingredients. Spread quickly on cookie sheet.
Let cool at room temperature and cut into bars.

"The best index to a person's character is how he treats
people who can't do him any good, and how he treats
people who can't fight back." -Abigail Van Buren

CHEWY FAT FREE MOOKIE
(Half way between a muffin and a cookie.)

3 eggs

2 cups brown sugar

1 ½ cups applesauce

2 teaspoons vanilla

2 cups flour

3 cups oatmeal

2 teaspoons baking powder

2 teaspoons baking soda

1 teaspoon salt

1 cup coconut

1 cup chocolate chips

1 cup raisins

1 cup dates

Beat together sugar and eggs. Stir in applesauce and vanilla. Mix flour, oatmeal, baking powder, baking soda and salt together. Add to the flour the coconut, chocolate chips, raisins and dates. Stir into the egg mixture. Drop cookies from a teaspoon onto a cookie sheet sprayed with vegetable oil. Bake at 350° F. for 11 minutes.

SPECIAL CONECAKES

(These look so great iced with pastel butter icing
and decorated with sprinkles.)

Have all ingredients at room temperature.

1¾ cups all-purpose flour

1¼ cup granulated sugar

2½ teaspoons baking powder

1 teaspoon salt

⅓ cup butter, softened

⅔ cup milk

1 egg

⅓ cup milk

1 teaspoon vanilla

20 flat-bottomed ice cream cones

Preheat oven to 375° F. Measure flour, baking powder and salt into small bowl. Add butter and milk, mix for 2 minutes at medium speed. Add and mix for another two minutes at medium speed: egg, milk and vanilla, scraping bowl constantly. Fill cones about ¾ full leaving the batter ½ inch from top. Place filled cones on a baking tray or in muffin pans. Bake in oven for about 25 to 30 minutes until an inserted wooden pick comes out clean.

SECRET MILK RECIPE
(Kids love this!)

½ cup water

¼ cup cinnamon red hots candy

¼ cup honey

1 tablespoon whole cloves

4 cups milk

In a saucepan stir together the water, candy, honey and cloves. Bring to a boil and simmer for 5 minutes. Strain out the cloves, Slowly stir in the milk and heat. Serves 6.

While attending a marriage seminar on communication, Wally, and his wife, Carolyn, listened to the instructor declare " It is essential that husbands and wives know the things that are important to each other." He addressed the man. "Can you describe your wife's favourite flower?" Wally leaned over, touched Carolyn's arm gently and whispered, "Robin Hood All-Purpose, isn't it?" And thus began Wally's life of celibacy

HOLLY WREATHS

(Easy to make and really dress up a children's tray of Christmas cookies)

½ cup butter
35 large marshmallows
½ teaspoon vanilla extract
1½ teaspoons green food colouring
3 ½ cups corn flakes
Small red cinnamon candies (1 to 2 tablespoons)

In large, heavy 2-quart saucepan, melt butter and marshmallows over low heat, stirring constantly. Add vanilla and food colouring and stir until well blended. Fold in corn flakes. Grease tablespoon. Drop by rounded tablespoonfuls onto waxed paper-lined cookie sheets; shape into 2-inch wreaths. (I use a wooden skewer to shape the wreath). Decorate each with cinnamon candies. Makes about 25 wreaths. * Greased muffin tins work well to shape wreaths.

PRIZEWINNING CARAMEL CORN

6 quarts popped corn

Syrup:
2 cups brown sugar
½ cup corn syrup
1 cup butter
¼ teaspoon cream of tartar
1 teaspoon salt
1 teaspoon baking soda

Boil above mixture except for baking soda, to 260° F. (hard ball). Remove and add baking soda. Pour over popped corn. Mix well. Put in large roaster and bake at 200° F. for 1 hour. Stir 3-4 times during this time.

"Once the game is over, the King and the pawn go back in the same box."   *Italian Proverb*

PUFFED WHEAT SQUARES

⅓ cup butter
1 cup corn syrup
¾ cup brown sugar
¼ cup peanut butter
1 teaspoon vanilla
2 teaspoons honey
8 cups puffed wheat

Melt butter in Dutch oven. Add next 5 ingredients. When this mixture comes to a boil, boil for about 2 minutes. Remove from heat and add puffed wheat. Stir well and pat down in a greased 9 x 13 inch cake pan. Cut after chilled.
* May substitute puffed rice for a variation.

"When the eagles are silent,
the parrots begin to jabber."
Sir William Churchill

RANCH NUTS AND BOLTS
(A Christmas treat or just a nutritious snack.)

1 package powdered ranch dressing
1 cup canola oil
2 tablespoons dill weed
1 ½ teaspoons garlic powder
1 box Crispex
1 bag pretzels
1 box Cheerios
1 bag Bugles
1 bag peanuts, salted
1 box Mini Ritz Crackers
1 bag Ranch Crispers

Mix all cereals, nuts and crackers together in a large container or bag. Blend oil mixture and spices (first four ingredients) and pour over dry mixture. Shake bag often or stir mixture throughout the day. Ready after cereal mixture is dry (usually about 24 hrs.)

An advantage of getting older is now when you decide to go bra-less, it pulls all the wrinkles out of your face.

GUMDROP POPCORN CAKE
(This makes a great gift for neighbors at Christmas.)

14 cups of popped popcorn
1 cup assorted nuts (we usually use peanuts and almond flakes)
1 pound marshmallows
½ cup canola oil
½ cup margarine
1 pound baking gumdrops

Melt margarine, add oil and marshmallows. Cook over low heat (or in the microwave) until marshmallows are melted. Stir to combine ingredients. Put popcorn, nuts and gumdrops in large bowl. Pour marshmallow mixture over popcorn and mix. Lightly grease an angel pan and pack mixture in firmly. Let harden and turn out. (If you have a nut allergy in the family...just add a few more gumdrops and leave out the nuts....still yummy!

"Who of you by worrying can add a single hour to his life?"   Matthew 6:25-27

GRANOLA BARS

3 cups oatmeal

1 cup Rice Krispies

2 tablespoons sesame seeds

1 cup nuts or sunflower seeds

½ cup chocolate chips

1 cup brown sugar

¾ cup syrup

1 cup peanut butter

½ cup margarine

Melt brown sugar, syrup, peanut butter and margarine and pour over dry ingredients.

Place mixture in 9 x 13 inch greased pan and bake for 15 to 20 minutes at 350° F. Cut into bars and individually wrap.

"The mind of the bigot is like the pupil of the eye; the more light you pour upon it, the more it will contract."
-- Oliver Wendell Holmes

TAKE ALONG BREAKFAST BARS

4 cups quick-cooking rolled oats (not instant)
2 cups medium unsweetened coconut
1 cup corn flakes cereal, lightly crushed
1 cup dried apricots, chopped
1 cup raisins
⅔ cup roasted sunflower seeds, shelled
½ cup hard margarine
1 -11 ounce can sweetened condensed milk
¼ cup corn syrup
2 teaspoons frozen concentrated orange juice

Combine first six ingredients in large bowl. Melt margarine in medium saucepan. Add remaining three ingredients. Heat and stir on low until combined. Pour over granola mixture while tossing. Mixture will be quite sticky. Pack firmly into two greased 9 x 13 inch pans. Bake in 325° F. oven for 20-30 minutes until edges are golden. Score while warm. Let cool on wire rack. Cut into 2 x 3 inch bars and warp individual bars in plastic wrap. Makes 30 bars.

Common equivalents

1 lb. powdered sugar = 2⅓ cups

1 lb. brown sugar = 2¼ cups firmly packed

1 lb. granulated sugar = 2 cups

½ lb. pkg. of unsweetened chocolate = 8 (one ounce) squares

3 ounce pkg. cream cheese = 6 tbsp.

1 lb. cottage cheese = 2 cups

1 lb. cheese = 4 cups grated

1 lb. butter = 2 cups

1 stick butter = ½ cup

½ pint whipping cream = 2 cups whipped

12 to 14 egg yolks = 1 cup

8 egg whites = about 1 cup

1 lb. peaches = 4 medium

1 medium orange = ⅓ cup juice

1 medium lemon = 3 tbsp. juice

1 lb. walnuts, shelled = 4 cups

¼ lb. marshmallows = 16 whole

11 graham crackers = 1 cup crumbs

1 lb. cake flour = 5 cups sifted

1 lb. all-purpose flour = 4 cups sifted

1 lb. dried prunes = 2½ cups

1 lb. cooked prunes = 4 cups

In Honour of
The Angels Among Us

Although you've left and now walk above
I'm never alone; I'm wrapped in your love
Enjoy now your long waited reward
Feel peace that your love continues on
What was taught to me,
will be taught to mine
Cause you live on in me even
after you've gone

AVRA'S FAVORITE SWEETS

(It was however, a rare occurrence that she ate
anything with so many calories!)

AVRA'S MOTHER-IN-LAW'S
PEANUT BUTTER SLICE

Heat until dissolved:

1 cup brown sugar

1 cup white syrup

Add:

2 cups peanut butter

2 cups rice krispies

4 cups corn flakes

Press in 9 x 13 inch cake pan.

Icing:

6 tablespoons cream

10 tablespoons brown sugar

4 tablespoons butter

2 cups icing sugar

Boil cream, sugar and butter for one minute. Add icing
sugar and beat well. Spread over cake.

AVRA'S KNISHES

(A Jewish dish. Knishes are served as a side
dish, in place of potatoes. They are delicious! The
dough after baking is similar to phyllo pastry.
You can also substitute cottage
cheese for potatoes.)

Filling:
Dutch oven full of potatoes, boiled and riced
2 large onions, chopped and fried in butter
Salt and pepper to taste
Mix together the potatoes, fried onions, salt and
pepper.
Dough:
1 egg, beaten
½ cup canola oil
½ cup warm water
1 teaspoon vinegar
1 teaspoon salt
2 cups flour
Mix together egg, oil, warm water, vinegar and
salt. Add flour. Mix well and make into 3 balls
and let sit for at least 1 hour. Pour a few
tablespoons of oil into a small bowl for brushing.
Roll out dough into a rectangle on lightly floured
surface as thin as possible. Dip pastry brush in
Continued on next page.............

AVRA'S KNISHES ....

oil and brush over rolled out dough. Put mashed
potato mixture along the edge of the dough; fold
in corners and roll tight. Use the side of your
hand to cut the knishes into 2-inch pieces. Place
knishes on cookie sheets and freeze. Pack into
zip-lock bags and keep frozen. Bake frozen
knishes at 350°F. for 30-40 minutes or until
golden brown. Serve with sour cream.

AVRA'S KOOGLE

(A Jewish dish similar to lasagna without meat.)
1 package broad egg noodles
1 -8 ounce carton sour cream
1 -8 ounce carton cottage cheese, creamed
¼ cup butter, melted
salt and pepper to taste
4 eggs, beaten
1 ½ cups cheddar cheese, grated
Boil noodles according to package directions.
Drain. Mix together; sour cream, cottage cheese,
butter, salt and pepper, eggs and cheddar cheese.
Add the noodles last. Pour into a greased
casserole dish and bake at 350° F. for 40
minutes.

AVRA'S CHEESECAKE CUPCAKES

1 package vanilla wafers
¾ cup sugar
3 -8 ounce packages cream cheese, softened
3 eggs, plus 2 additional egg whites
1 tablespoon lemon juice
1 teaspoon vanilla
pie filling or fresh fruit for topping

Blend in food processor sugar, cream cheese, eggs, lemon juice and vanilla until smooth. Line cupcake pans with 24 medium-sized paper cups. Place 1 vanilla wafer in bottom of each cup. Spoon cheese mixture over wafers to fill cups ¾ full. Bake in 350°F. oven for 18-20 minutes. Cool cupcakes. Spoon pie filling on each cupcake and refrigerate.
Optional: Top each cupcake with whipped cream and fresh fruit.

"The fragrance always stays in the hand that gives the rose." Heda Bejar

366

AVRA'S PECAN SQUARES

1 cup flour
¼ cup brown sugar
½ cup butter
Mix and pat into 9 x 13 inch pan and bake for 10
minutes at 350° F.

Combine and cook for 5 minutes:
½ cup butter
1 cup maple syrup
⅔ cup brown sugar
2 tablespoons flour

Add: 2 beaten eggs
1 teaspoon vanilla
¾ cup pecans
Spread over baked crust and sprinkle with pecans. Bake
for 30 minutes at 350°F.

*"I generally avoid temptation unless I
can't resist it."*   Mae West

AVRA'S ORANGE POPPYSEED CHEESE CAKE WITH RASPBERRY SAUCE

Crust:
1 cup blanched almonds, crushed
6 tablespoons butter
1 cup graham crumbs
1 tablespoon sugar

Melt butter, add remaining ingredients and press into sprayed 10 inch springform pan. Bake 8 minutes at 350° F.

Filling:
3 packages (8 ounces) cream cheese, softened
1½ tablespoons orange peel, grated
1 cup sugar
¼ cup butter, melted
½ cup sour cream
1 teaspoon vanilla
3½ tablespoons orange juice
4 large eggs
2 tablespoons poppy seed
Beat cream cheese, sugar, butter and orange peel. Add sour cream, orange juice and vanilla until blended.
Continued on next page.............

AVRA'S ORANGE POPPYSEED CHEESE CAKE
WITH RASPBERRY SAUCE continued.........

Add eggs 1 at a time. Mix in poppy seed. Pour over crust. Bake 20 minutes at 350°F. and reduce oven to 300°F. and bake another 20 minutes. Reduce oven to 250°F. and bake until barely set in centre, approximately 45 minutes.

Topping:
1½ cups sour cream
1½ tablespoons sugar
2 tablespoons orange juice

Blend. Pour over cake. Increase oven to 350° F. Bake for 8 minutes until just set. Refrigerate overnight.

Raspberry Sauce:
4 cups frozen raspberries
6 tablespoons sugar
¼ cup orange juice

Puree raspberries, add sugar and orange juice. Can be prepared a day ahead. Spoon over each piece of cheesecake as you serve it.

HAZEL'S JELLY ROLL

6 egg yolks
½ cup boiling water
1 teaspoon baking powder
1 teaspoon vanilla
1 cup white sugar
½ teaspoon salt
1 ½ cups sifted cake flour
jam or jelly of your choice

Beat egg yolks until thick and lemony. Add sugar and
continue beating, then add water. Add remaining
ingredients and beat for two minutes. Pour into a jelly
roll pan lined with wax paper. Bake for 25 minutes at
350°F. Roll while hot, fill with jelly.
*Variation – prepare lemon pie filling and use as
substitute for jelly.

*"Sorrow makes us all children again- destroys all
differences of intellect. The wisest know nothing."*
Ralph W. Emerson

HAZEL'S SWEET AND SOUR MEATBALLS
(with Rice Krispies)

1½ pounds ground beef

2 cups Rice Krispies

½ cup onions, chopped

1 teaspoon salt

1 teaspoon pepper

1 egg

Sauce:

¾ cup sugar

¼ cup vinegar

2 cups water

2 teaspoons soya sauce

2 teaspoons flour

1 -14 ounce can pineapple tidbits (optional)

Mix ground beef, Rice Krispies, onion, salt, pepper, and egg. Shape into small balls (walnut size) and brown. Mix the sauce ingredients and pour over the meatballs. Simmer for ½ hour and serve with rice.

HAZEL'S SWEET DOUGH CRESCENTS

2 tablespoons fast rising yeast

½ cup lukewarm water

2 teaspoons sugar

1 cup milk

¾ cup sugar

2 teaspoons salt

¾ cup cold water

½ cup shortening

3 eggs, beaten

7 cups flour

Soak yeast in ½ cup of warm water and 2 teaspoons sugar. Let set for 10 minutes. Add all other ingredients to make a soft dough. Cover and let rise for 1 hour. Knead down, and let rise another hour. Grease baking sheet. Divide dough into 4 or 5 balls. Roll ball of dough with greased rolling pin into circular shape about ¼ inch thick. Cut in 12 pie shaped pieces. Brush with melted butter. Sprinkle with a little brown sugar and a dash of cinnamon. Roll up beginning at the wide end. Seal point to bun. Place on baking sheet and curve in crescents. Brush tops with melted butter, cover and let rise at room temperature for about 1 ½ hours. Bake at 375° F. for 20 minutes. Turn out on wire racks. Cool and ice with white icing. Makes 5 dozen rolls.

OLGA'S CABBAGE ROLLS

Filling:

1 pound hamburger, thawed

2 cups rice, partially cooked

2 eggs

2 teaspoons salt

1 teaspoon pepper

1 medium onion, chopped

1 head cabbage leaves, boiled to soften

3 -10 ounce cans tomato soup

3 -10 ounce cans water

Mix together hamburger, partially cooked rice, eggs, salt, pepper and onions. Place heaping tablespoon of filling onto cabbage leaf (hard core removed) and roll up, tucking in ends. Place in lightly sprayed roaster in layers on top of each other. Blend the tomato soup and water and pour over. Cover. Bake in a 350°F. oven for 2 hours or until cabbage is tender.

*Cabbage rolls can be frozen separately on a cookie sheet, then put into plastic bags and taken out as needed. One thing to note, the cabbage is tougher when frozen so will need to be baked longer.

OLGA'S CREAM CHEESE SQUARES
(So easy but so good.)

1 ¼ cups graham wafer crumbs

¼ cup margarine, melted

1 -8 ounce package cream cheese

½ cup sugar

1 egg

1 teaspoon vanilla

1 teaspoon lemon juice

Mix together the graham wafer crumbs and margarine. Press ¾ of the mixture into the bottom of a 9 x 9 inch pan. Beat together the cream cheese, sugar, egg, vanilla and lemon juice. Pour over crumb mixture. Cover with remaining crumbs. Bake in a 325°F. oven for 20 minutes.

"Happiness is a wonderful commodity, the more you give, the more you have." Voltaire

OLGA'S HOT MILK CAKE
(This cake tastes best when it's warm.)

1 cup flour
1 cup sugar
2 eggs
1 ¼ teaspoons baking powder
1 teaspoon vanilla

Bring to a boil:
½ cup milk
2 tablespoons margarine

Mix dry ingredients with hot mixture. Pour in a 9 x 9 inch greased pan. Bake at 350°F. for 30 minutes.

Topping:
5 tablespoons brown sugar
3 tablespoons margarine, melted
2 tablespoons cream
½ cup coconut
Mix topping ingredients together and spread over hot cake. Return to oven and bake until topping is bubbly, about 3 minutes.

OLGA'S MALL DALCHEN
(Very yummy!)

2 eggs	1 cup milk
½ teaspoon salt	2¾ cups flour
½ cup sugar	1 teaspoon cinnamon

1 ½ cups heavy cream, approximately

Knead eggs, milk, salt and flour together to make a sticky dough. Roll half of the dough on floured surface to ⅛ inch thick. Spread a very thin layer of cream over dough. Sprinkle with ¼ cup sugar and ½ teaspoon cinnamon. Roll like a jelly roll, folding the edges in to seal in the cream mixture. Place in a 9 x 13 inch, greased pan. Repeat with other half of the dough, using the other ¼ cup sugar and ½ teaspoon cinnamon and place in the same pan. Sprinkle ¼ cup sugar and a bit of cinnamon on top. Pour 1 ½ cups heavy cream over rolls. The rolls should be half covered with liquid. Bake at 350°F. for 1 hour or until most of liquid is gone.

Variation: Place thinly sliced apples, cooked prunes, raisins or your favorite fruit over the cream, sugar and cinnamon mixture in the centre of the roll.

OLGA'S PASTA AND LETTUCE SALAD

1 cup macaroni, cooked
½ head iceberg lettuce, torn
4 eggs, hard-boiled and sliced
2 green onions, chopped
Dressing:
1 cup salad dressing
3 tablespoons sugar
1 tablespoon vinegar
1 teaspoon prepared mustard
Mix dressing and pour over salad mixture.

OLGA'S KUCKAN

(When you make a batch of buns, use some of your
dough to make a loaf of this!)

¾ cup sugar
3 eggs
1 cup heavy cream
cinnamon, sprinkle
Mix in a bowl the sugar, eggs and cream. Grease a
loaf pan. Pour in ⅓ of above mixture. Place shaped
loaf of dough on top. Pour remaining cream, mixture
over dough. Sprinkle with cinnamon. Let rise and bake
at 350°F. for about 20 minutes or until done.

OLGA'S PUMPKIN PIE

(For a lighter dessert this can be served as a pudding.)

1 tablespoon flour
½ teaspoon salt
¼ cup brown sugar
¼ cup honey
¼ teaspoon of each: ginger, mace and nutmeg
1 teaspoon cinnamon
1 tablespoon margarine, melted
1 cup milk
2 eggs, beaten
1 ½ cups pumpkin

Mix all together and pour into an unbaked pie shell. Bake at 450° F. for 10 minutes. Reduce heat to 325° F. Bake for approximately 40 minutes or until an inserted knife comes out clean.

"Time is:
Too short for those who wait
Too swift for those who fear
Too long for those who grieve
Too short for those who rejoice
But for those who love, time is eternity."
Henry Van Dyke

REENA'S CHILI

1 pound hamburger

1 onion, chopped

1 can tomato sauce

1 can kidney beans

1 can brown beans

2 cans mushrooms, sliced

Brown the hamburger. Add the rest of the ingredients. Sprinkle chili powder over, stir, repeat once or twice. Let it simmer. Serve with grated cheese and steamed rice.

"The better part of one's life consists of his friendships." Abraham Lincoln

REENA'S FROZEN PINEAPPLE DELIGHT

2 cups graham wafer crumbs, crushed
¼ cup butter, melted
½ cup soft butter
1¼ cups icing sugar
2 eggs
1 teaspoon vanilla
1 cup whipping cream, whipped
1 -20 ounce can crushed pineapple

Combine crumbs and melted butter. Place all but ½
cup crumbs in 9 x 12 inch pan and press down.
Cream butter, gradually adding icing sugar. Add eggs,
one at a time and beat until smooth. Add vanilla and
spread mixture over crumbs in the pan. Whip cream
until stiff and combine with well-drained pineapple.
Spread over top of second layer. Sprinkle remaining
crumbs on top. Store in freezer. Serve frozen.

"What can't be cured must be endured."
Old English Proverb

REENA'S LASAGNA

7 lasagna noodles
1 large onion, chopped
½ teaspoon garlic powder
2 -14 ounce can tomato sauce
1 pound Italian mozzerella cheese
1 pound ground beef
2 tablespoons canola oil
1 can mushrooms
salt and pepper to taste

Brown onion with garlic powder in oil. Add ground beef. Cook until done. Add mushrooms and tomato sauce. Season to taste. Simmer slowly for 20 minutes. Cook lasagna as directed on package. Drain, chill in cold water. Arrange 1 layer of cooked lasagna in parallel strips on greased baking dish (11 X 7 inch) Cover with hamburger mixture. Top with slices of cheese. Repeat layers until all ingredients used. Bake in 375° F. for 30 minutes. Let stand 10 minutes before cutting into servings.

REENA'S LEMON MERINGUE PIE

8 inch baked pie shell
1 cup sugar
¼ cup cornstarch
1 cup water
2 egg yolks, slightly beaten
2 tablespoons margarine or butter
1 teaspoon lemon peel, grated
⅓ cup lemon juice
2 drops yellow food colouring (optional)

Bake pie shell. Heat oven to 400° F. Mix sugar and cornstarch in 1½ quart saucepan. Stir in water gradually. Cook over medium heat, stirring constantly, until mixture thickens and boils. Boil and stir 1 minute. Stir at least half of the hot mixture gradually into egg yolks. Blend back into hot mixture in saucepan. Boil and stir 1 minute. Remove from heat; stir in margarine, lemon peel, lemon juice and food colouring. Pour into pie shell.

Meringue for pie continued on next page.....

MERINGUE

2 egg whites   ¼ teaspoon cream of tarter
¼ cup sugar   ¼ teaspoon vanilla
Beat egg whites and cream of tarter until foamy. Beat
in sugar, 1 tablespoon at a time; continue beating
until stiff and glossy. Do not under beat. Beat in
vanilla. Spoon meringue onto hot pie filling. Spread
over filling; carefully sealing meringue to edge of crust
to prevent shrinking or weeping. Bake until delicate
brown, about 10 minutes. Cool.

REENA'S TACO SPREAD

8-ounce package cream cheese, softened
½ cup sour cream
¼ cup mayonnaise
1 small jar of seafood cocktail sauce
2 cups cheddar cheese, shredded
2 green onions, chopped
1 tomato, diced.
1 cup lettuce, shredded
3 cans broken shrimp, rinsed and drained (optional)
Mix cream cheese, sour cream, and mayonnaise
together. Spread over a 12 inch pizza pan.
Layer: shrimp, lettuce, tomato, onions, and top with
cheese. Serve with assorted crackers.

REENA'S SWEET AND SOUR MEATBALLS

1 pound ground beef
½ pound ground pork
1 pound ground ham or 2 cans flakes of ham
1 package dry onion soup mix
2 eggs
1½ cup crushed cracker crumbs
½ can evaporated milk
Mix ingredients really well. No other seasonings
required. Form into small meat balls. These freeze well.

SWEET AND SOUR SAUCE

¾ cup vinegar
1½ cups brown sugar
1 teaspoon dry mustard
2 tablespoons soya sauce
3 cups hot water
Mix well and pour over meatballs. Bake uncovered in
350° F. oven for 2 hours. Stir several times.

REENA'S SPECIALTY NO BAKE CHEESECAKE

1 -9 ounce package of cream cheese

1 tin of cherry pie filling

1 package of dream whip

2 cups graham wafers, crushed

4 tablespoons white sugar

½ teaspoon cinnamon

½ cup butter, melted

Mix crumbs, sugar, melted butter and cinnamon and press into and 8 x 8 inch pan. Reserve some of the crumb mixture to sprinkle on top later. Place in a 350° F. oven for 10 minutes.

Whip cream cheese in mix master. Whip dream whip according to instructions. Then combine the two. Spread on top of cooled crust. Cover with cherry pie filling. Sprinkle top with remaining crust.

"Children are the hands by which we take hold of heaven." Henry Ward Beecher

Because we are old-fashioned cooks you will notice that the recipes in this book are given in Imperial measurements. For anyone that has converted to metric, we are sorry.

Hope this helps you out!

Oven Temperatures

250°F = 120°C
275°F = 140°C
300°F = 150°C
325°F = 160°C
350°F = 180°C   Slow oven . 250°F – 325°F
375°F = 190°C   Moderate ... 325°F - 375°F
400°F = 200°C   Hot ....425°F - 450°F
425°F = 220°C
450°F = 230°C
500°F = 260°C

Volume

¼ teaspoon = 1 ml
½ teaspoon = 2 ml
1 teaspoon = 5 ml
1 tablespoon = 15 ml
¼ cup = 50 ml
⅓ cup = 75 ml
½ cup = 125 ml
⅔ cup = 150 ml
¾ cup = 175 ml
1 cup = 250 ml

Weight

1 ounce = 30 g
2 ounce = 55 g
3 ounces = 85 g
4 ounces = 115 g
5 ounces = 140 g
6 ounces = 170 g
7 ounces = 200 g
8 ounces = 250 g
16 ounces = 500 g
32 ounces = 1000 g

I N D E X

VEGETABLE & SIDE DISHES

DESSERTS

ANGELS AMONG US

Canola Oil

You will notice that many of the recipes in this book are made using canola oil. Why canola?

Canola is the combination of two words - Canadian and oil. It is produced by crushing seed from Canada's own oilseed crop - Canola. Nutritional research has focused upon the role of fats and oils in the human diet. Recent developments have shown canola oil to be the edible oil of choice in a "heart-healthy" diet. In *Breasts of Friends* we chose canola oil for its nutritional attributes as it contains the lowest level of saturated fatty acids of any vegetable oil. It is high in monounsaturated fatty acids, which have been shown to reduce blood cholesterol levels, and has moderate levels of essential polyunsaturated fatty acids, It is also a rich source of vitamin E. Like all vegetable oils, canola oil is cholesterol-free.

   Nutritional Analysis-(Analysis for refined canola oil)

10 mL (2 tsp.)

83 calories

9.2 g fat

0.6 g saturated fatty acids

5.8 g monounsaturated fatty acids

2.0 g linoleic fatty acid (omega - 6)

0.8 g alpha-linolenic fatty acid (omega - 3)

No trace of cholesterol

1.9 mg Vitamin E

A Gift of Hope
Order Form
For the Breasts of Friends
Box 436
Foam Lake, SK Canada
SOA 1AO

Please send me _____ copies of <u>For the Breasts of Friends</u> at $19.95 each plus $5.00 (total order up to 5 books, $10.00 for 5 to 10 books) for mailing. Over 10 books call or email to make shipping arrangements). Canadian residents add 7% G.S.T. Net profits go to Breast Cancer Agencies. See our website for a list of agencies that have received donations.

Name _____

Street or Box_____

City, Province_____

Country, Postal Code (Zip code)_____

Make cheques payable to Breast Friends.
The book can also be ordered by calling 1-877-723-6828 or by email at <u>breastfriends@sasktel.net</u> . The website www.breastfriends.ca features the book — some recipes, more information and an ordering link.